Joys
of
Fantasy

The Book for

By SIV CEDERING FOX

Photographs by
JOSEPH DEL VALLE
Director of Photography,
ED ROTHKOWITZ

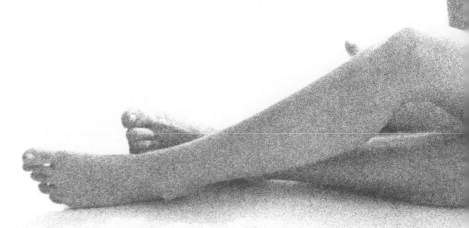

Joys of Fantasy

Loving Couples

BELL PUBLISHING COMPANY
NEW YORK

Library of Congress Cataloging in Publication Data
Fox, Siv Cedering.
   Joys of fantasy.

   Reprint. Originally published: New York:
Stein and Day, 1977.
   1. Erotic poetry, American. I. Title.
PS3556.0955J6 1982   811'.54   82-1346
                  AACR2

ISBN: 0-517-362473

h g f e d c b a

Sometimes
I told myself very
adventurous love-stories
with myself as hero

W.B. YEATS
Autobiographies

Joys of Fantasy

Everybody's Doing It

Some overgrown zucchini were brought into the office. All the women giggled. A bowl full of apples or potatoes would not give the same effect. Neither would grapes, tomatoes, or lettuce. But a big banana, cucumber, or zucchini can be a cause for hilarity.

The women who giggle at overgrown zucchini might deny that they have sexual fantasies. If you asked them: "Have you ever imagined making love to, or masturbating with, a zucchini?" most of them would probably say No. If they were prodded, they might admit that they do see a similarity, which they find amusing, between the vegetable and an overgrown penis. Whether they admit it or not, their thoughts, which are their fantasies, do see the zucchini as a sexual object that could

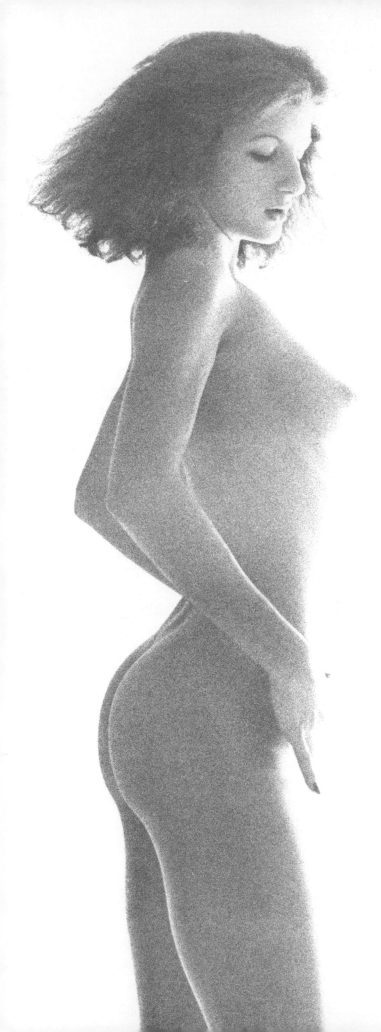

enter them. When they giggle at the overgrown zucchini, they are giggling at the idea of making love to a thing of such unusual proportions. They are fantasizing.

The truth of the matter is that everybody fantasizes. If you ever have finished a thought like *When I get rich* . . . or *When I get married* . . . or *If I could spend a night alone with* . . . , you are fantasizing. And it is good to fantasize. Imagination is a necessary ingredient in hope and wish, prayer and desire. It can build anticipation and deepen delight. The happy daydreams that drift around a relationship are the very magic of that relationship. One can say that the mind is the main erogenous zone. It is there sense becomes sensuality.

We start to fantasize as children and continue through our lives. Our first sexual fantasies might start like this:

*I wonder what it would feel like
to kiss Marilyn.*

Would Billy laugh if I touched his hand?

*I wonder how it would feel to touch a
pair of bare breasts . . .*

*If I go to the dance with Johnny, and he
kisses me . . .*

*If I get to borrow the car, and Annie comes
for a ride, and we stop on the way home,
and . . .*

What if daddy wanted to make love to me?

During puberty a lot of time is spent
imagining sensual and sexual encounters,
and the tone of a person's adult fantasies
might be set at that time. A girl who
dreams of a picture-book romance
followed by a fancy wedding might
continue to dream of her Prince Charming

when she is a married woman and mother of six. For daydreams continue through our adult lives.

What if some strange man broke into the house while Ben is gone and . . .

When I get my furlough, I'm gonna find the hottest cathouse, and . . .

If Johnny comes home . . .

If I ever get out of this town . . .

If I could only get Irene alone for a moment . . .

 HOT MOON

tonight i'm a lusty
old broad, sitting
on a bar stool
fat ass overhanging

bellowing old love songs,
beer foaming down chin
laughing, swaying hot

one of the guys around the bar
will later warm my bed

tomorrow
i will be a quiet virgin
quivering mutely

but tonight,

ah ha!
tonight i'm lusty,
an old broad
baying love songs
at the moon

M. EKOLA GERBERICK

 Dreaming Awake

Whether we remember our dreams when we awake or not, all of us do dream, and that dreaming is essential. It has been proved that a sure way to drive someone insane is to consistently deprive him of his dream time. During our waking hours a lot of time is spent solving problems, planning, learning, teaching. As a diversion from these systematic mental processes, we seem to need and enjoy some informal thinking: daydreaming.

Daydreams can happen anytime and anyplace—as we ride a train or plane and look out the window, as we look up from our work at the desk, as we are talking to people or reading a book. We are awake, but our thoughts move off into realms where everything is possible. It is a kind of relaxation for the brain. Instead of demanding a coffee break and extending it with a cigarette or a stick of Doublemint gum, the mind demands the freedom to daydream. The dreamer's thoughts can float from scene to thought to unanswered question to wish. If the dream has a story that perhaps is complete with details of colors, names, and sounds, it is a fantasy.

In our daydreams and fantasies we tend to imagine ourselves in pleasurable situations. We hope and imagine the hope fulfilled. We replay memories that are enjoyable. Like our night dreams, our daydreams can include fantasies that frighten us, or memories that sadden us or fill us with shame. If a disproportionate amount of a person's daydreaming is negative and frightening, he or she might need psychiatric help, just like the person whose night dreams are disturbing. But the happy daydreams, the memories that give pleasure and the fantasies that add excitement to the day, are healthy and normal in every way.

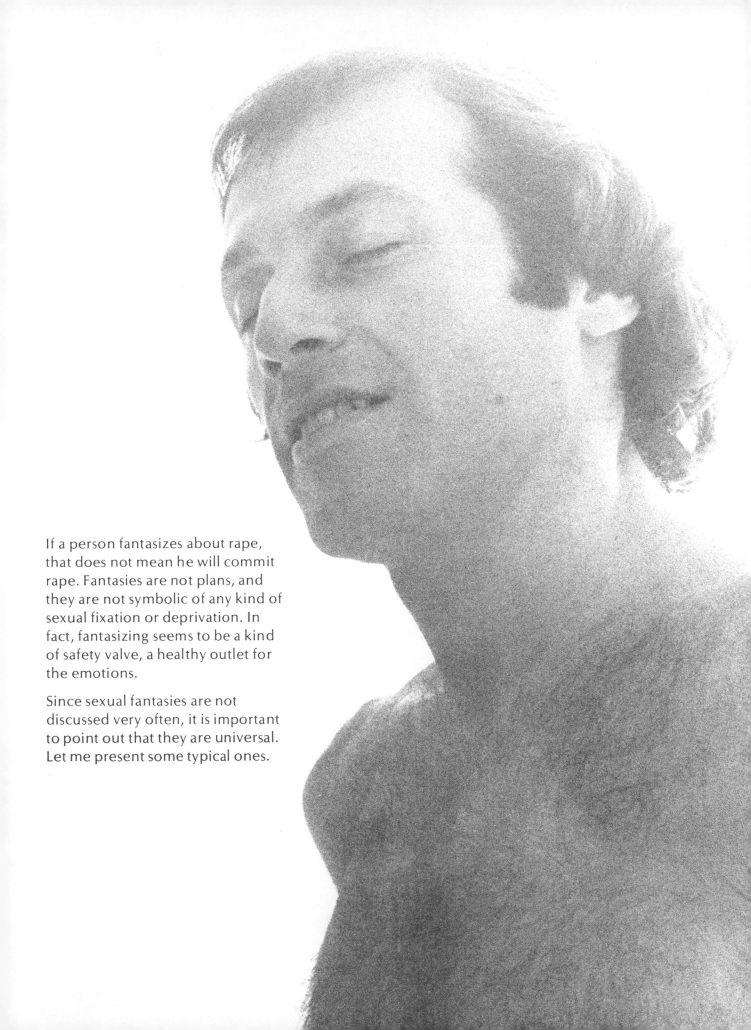

If a person fantasizes about rape, that does not mean he will commit rape. Fantasies are not plans, and they are not symbolic of any kind of sexual fixation or deprivation. In fact, fantasizing seems to be a kind of safety valve, a healthy outlet for the emotions.

Since sexual fantasies are not discussed very often, it is important to point out that they are universal. Let me present some typical ones.

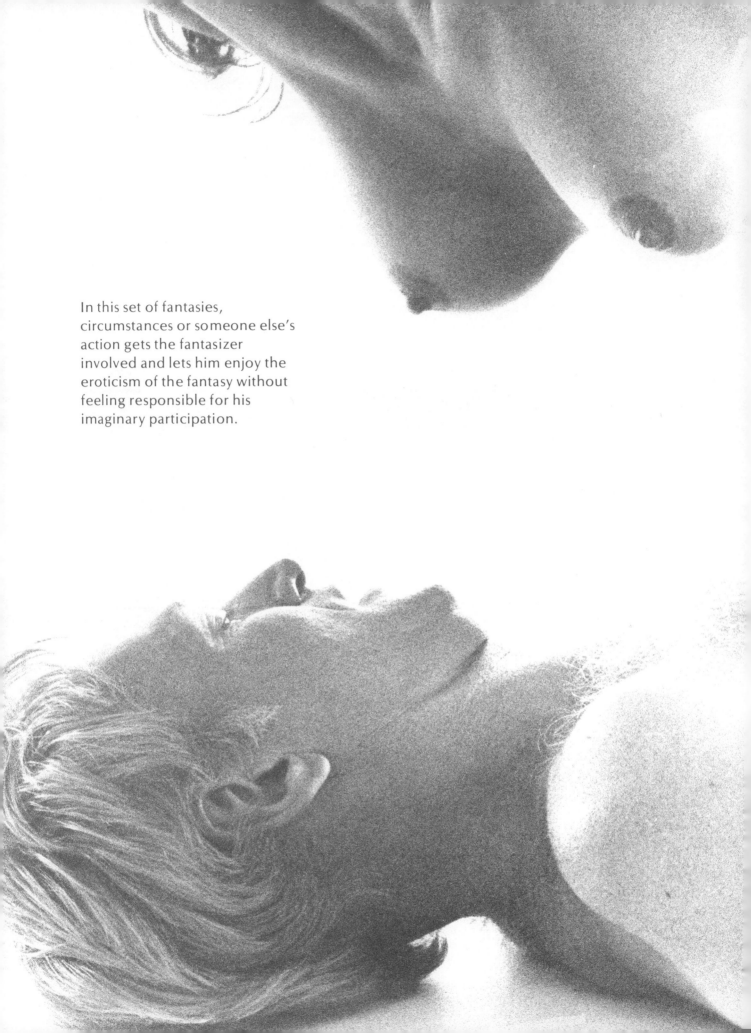

In this set of fantasies,
circumstances or someone else's
action gets the fantasizer
involved and lets him enjoy the
eroticism of the fantasy without
feeling responsible for his
imaginary participation.

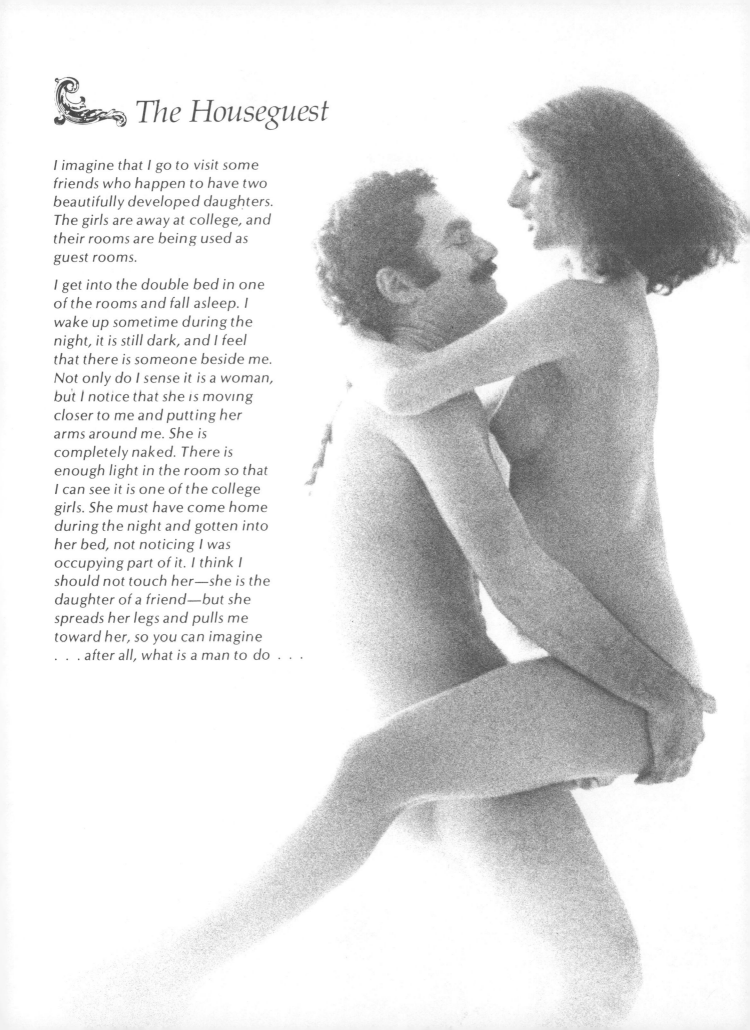

The Houseguest

I imagine that I go to visit some friends who happen to have two beautifully developed daughters. The girls are away at college, and their rooms are being used as guest rooms.

I get into the double bed in one of the rooms and fall asleep. I wake up sometime during the night, it is still dark, and I feel that there is someone beside me. Not only do I sense it is a woman, but I notice that she is moving closer to me and putting her arms around me. She is completely naked. There is enough light in the room so that I can see it is one of the college girls. She must have come home during the night and gotten into her bed, not noticing I was occupying part of it. I think I should not touch her—she is the daughter of a friend—but she spreads her legs and pulls me toward her, so you can imagine . . . after all, what is a man to do . . .

 *The Victim*

Another common fantasy is that of the victim. Here, again, the fantasizer gets into a sexual encounter she did not plan and cannot control. In this case, the fantasizer imagines herself forced into the act.

I think this when I am in bed with Jack. He knows I do it—we talk about it sometimes.

I imagine that I have been out late, and as I walk home, I notice a man following me. He tries to talk to me, but I walk on quickly. When I get to my building, he catches up with me. I get the key out of my pocketbook and open the door, and as I enter the foyer, he forces himself in. And then he grabs me.

I consider screaming, but I am afraid to wake the kids. I wouldn't want them to see what is happening. I try to fight him off, but pretty soon I notice I like what he is doing. He is rough, but he doesn't hurt me. He touches my breasts and rubs my thighs and pulls at my skirt and grabs me between the legs and pulls my panties aside, and in he goes. I am riding on his hips and he is pushing away and I am leaning against the wall and it is great.

By this time, Jack and I are really going at it. After we are done, he sort of teases me—in a nice way—and asks what I was imagining. Jack likes the fact that I like him to be a bit rough. Sometimes he talks to me as if he really is some kind of rapist. I guess we play the game together.

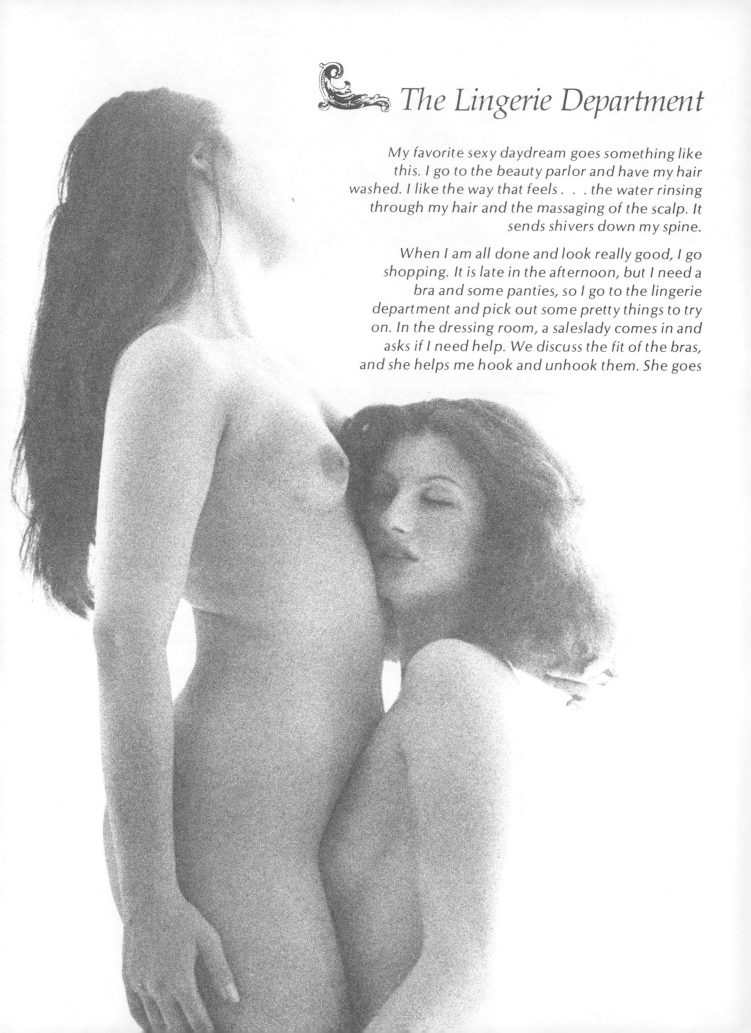

The Lingerie Department

My favorite sexy daydream goes something like this. I go to the beauty parlor and have my hair washed. I like the way that feels . . . the water rinsing through my hair and the massaging of the scalp. It sends shivers down my spine.

When I am all done and look really good, I go shopping. It is late in the afternoon, but I need a bra and some panties, so I go to the lingerie department and pick out some pretty things to try on. In the dressing room, a saleslady comes in and asks if I need help. We discuss the fit of the bras, and she helps me hook and unhook them. She goes

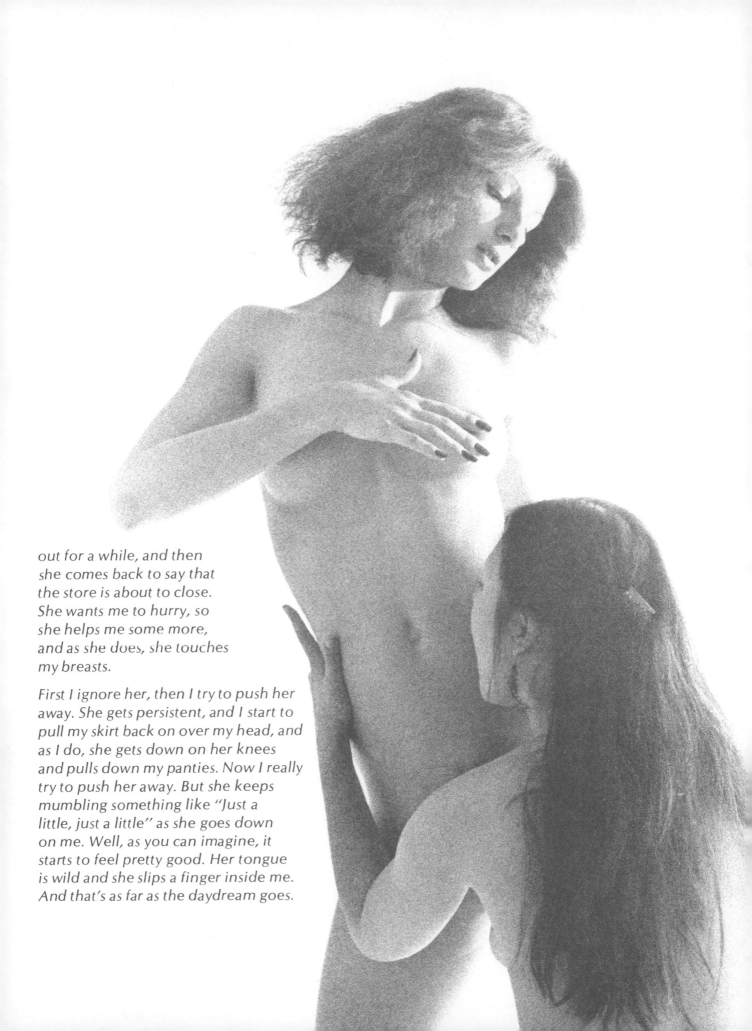

out for a while, and then she comes back to say that the store is about to close. She wants me to hurry, so she helps me some more, and as she does, she touches my breasts.

First I ignore her, then I try to push her away. She gets persistent, and I start to pull my skirt back on over my head, and as I do, she gets down on her knees and pulls down my panties. Now I really try to push her away. But she keeps mumbling something like "Just a little, just a little" as she goes down on me. Well, as you can imagine, it starts to feel pretty good. Her tongue is wild and she slips a finger inside me. And that's as far as the daydream goes.

The Football Hero

We have a coed football team at our school, and I am one of the six girls who show up for practice. We have a lot of fun, and sometimes we play way into the evenings. One evening, one of the girls caught the ball and ran with it and was tackled, and all of us ended up in a big heap of bodies on the ground. We lingered there longer than necessary, and I felt someone touch one of my breasts. There was even some kissing. We joked about it later, and that was that.

I really liked being in that heap of sweaty bodies, and I sometimes embellish the scene in my head. I imagine that I am the only girl who shows up for practice, and somehow or other all of us end up in a pile on the ground, and before I know it, the guys are pulling at my suit. They are pretty rough, and I get scared. I try to joke my fear away and say: "Hey, guys, I'll give you the ball." But the smart aleck of the bunch says: "Ball? We're gonna ball you."

I try to holler, but a guy who always has seemed pretty much of a prude puts his hand over my mouth and gets on top of me. I try to get away, but someone pulls the hand away from my mouth and starts to kiss me so hard I can hardly breathe,

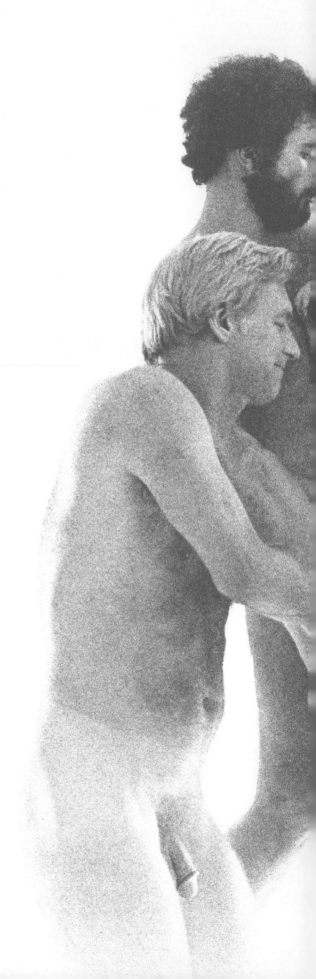

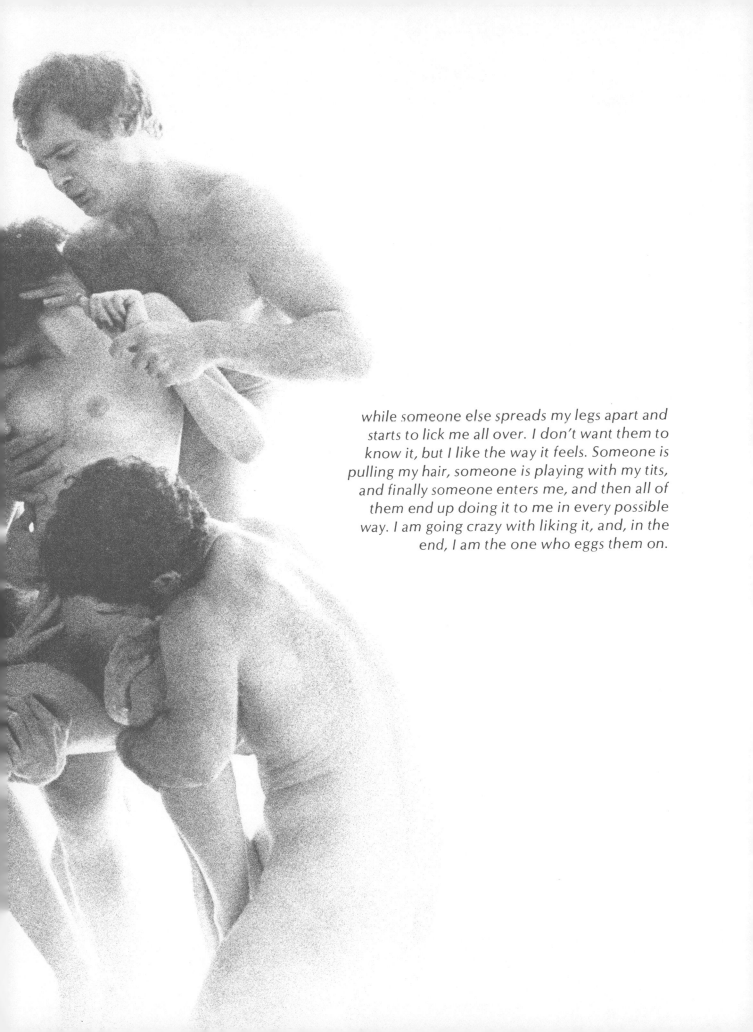

while someone else spreads my legs apart and starts to lick me all over. I don't want them to know it, but I like the way it feels. Someone is pulling my hair, someone is playing with my tits, and finally someone enters me, and then all of them end up doing it to me in every possible way. I am going crazy with liking it, and, in the end, I am the one who eggs them on.

 *Bathing Beauty*

I often go to the beach by myself; that way, I can get totally involved with the sounds of the water and the feel of the sun. The beach seems to be a good place for daydreams, too, and when I am there, or when I am some other place but thinking about the beach, I make up stories like this:

I am lying on the beach and I have just oiled myself. It is very sunny. My bathing suit top is untied so all of my back can get tan. As I lie there in the sun, I suddenly sense that someone has come between the sun and me.

I turn my head and see this beautifully tanned blond guy standing there. He is polite and says something like "Mind if I join you?"

I feel sun-grogged and lazy, so I don't put up a fight. He lies down beside me, and we exchange a word or two. I tell him I was almost asleep, so he says: "Go ahead and sleep, I'm sort of tired myself." But neither of us goes to sleep.

He moves closer and closer. He says something about the oil on my skin and starts to knead my back. Pretty soon, he is all hands and all over me.

We don't say much, but we exchange smiles and little moans. By this time, he has the biggest hard-on. I can't help touching it. He says: "Inside," and I slip my hand inside his bathing suit, and by this time he is really wiggling. We look around the beach—which luckily is pretty empty—and then we get under the blanket I have been lying on, and we pull our bathing suits off. Some people come walking down the beach, and we have to stop our motions. We pretend to be sleeping, but he is really inside me, and we flex our sex muscles and move imperceptibly. This is the part I like best."

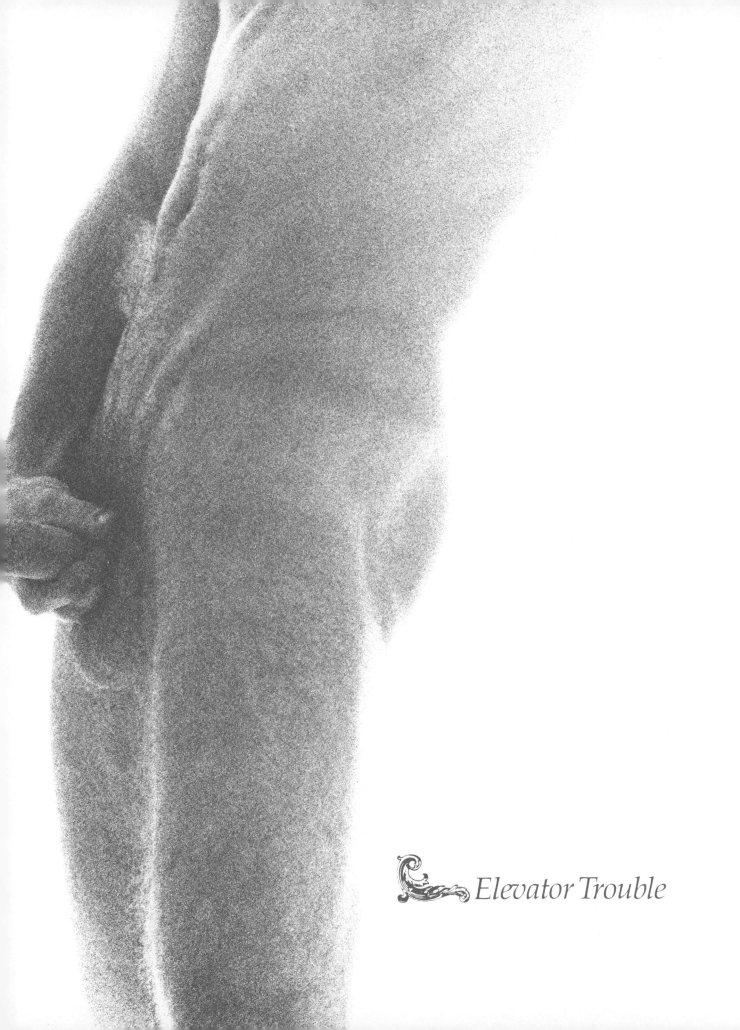

Elevator Trouble

This is Roger's story:

Remember the New York blackout? Well, this fantasy really started then. I was one of those who got stuck in an elevator. It was just for a few minutes, but it was long enough to give me material for one of my favorite fantasies.

There were four guys and two girls in the elevator. As I stood there with my attaché case, I suddenly felt a gentle jab in the groin. Then I heard a formal "I'm sorry" in a man's voice. I still don't know if someone touched me on purpose, or if somebody's briefcase had touched me, or what. It was dark, and we were trying to push whatever elevator button or emergency switch we could find.

That's all that actually happened, but in my fantasy it continues. I and one other guy get stuck in an elevator. He is younger than I, about nineteen or so. It is suddenly dark, and we are suspended somewhere between the thirty-fourth floor and the street. We try to push the emergency buttons, and I feel his hand on my prick. He apologizes, and I say: "It's okay." He takes that as a come-on and grabs me. I try to be cool and say something like "You must have misunderstood," but he isn't listening, he just keeps on rubbing me through my suit. Pretty soon, his other hand comes up to my face and sort of slithers around my head and my neck and through my hair, and he starts kissing me. I have only made it with a guy once, and that sort of scared me, but in this elevator scene I really like it. The sexiest part is the way it surprises me—I mean, the heat of it sort of flows over me, although I don't expect it.

There are various endings to this fantasy. At times the guy unzips me right there and gives me a blow job like I have never had before. He sucks and licks me, and I move in and out of his mouth, and he sticks his finger up my ass. In some versions, I fuck him in the ass and he fucks mine, and sometimes we just stand there and hold onto each other. At times, I imagine the light going on and the elevator doors opening, and we somehow manage to look respectable and leave the elevator with our flies closed and our attaché cases locked. Sometimes the doors open before anything happens, and as he leaves, I follow him home.

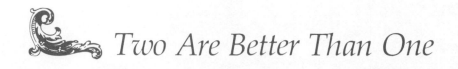 # Two Are Better Than One

My wife has a very pretty sister. She is as tall and well shaped as my wife, and their facial features are similar, but the surprising fact is that one of them is as dark as the other is blond. They are very close and affectionate with each other, and we laugh and joke a lot when the three of us are together. I have imagined us in bed together more than once.

The fantasy starts off slowly—we are lounging around the living-room floor, talking and teasing. I tell them I'll rub their backs, and they lie down on either side of me. I rub their shoulders and butts and the backs of their necks. I ask them to turn over, and I let my fingers trace their features and I knead their breasts gently. They are obviously enjoying it.

After a while, they say it's their turn, and I lie down on my stomach and they massage my back and arms. One of them runs her fingers around one of my ears, pulls at the lobe, and starts to lick it. The other one massages a hand and sucks at my fingers. Soon, they turn me over, and before too long we are all undressed and they rub me, caress me, tickle me with their hair, and scratch me.

At first they avoid my prick, but it is standing up pretty firmly by then, and my wife can't resist, so she starts sucking it. Her sister sticks her tongue into my mouth and goes wild kissing me. Then they trade off. It's wonderful to feel and to watch. Four hands, two mouths, the movement of blond hair and dark hair, and then the two cunts, one familiar and covered with reddish-blond hair, the other furry-dark and foreign.

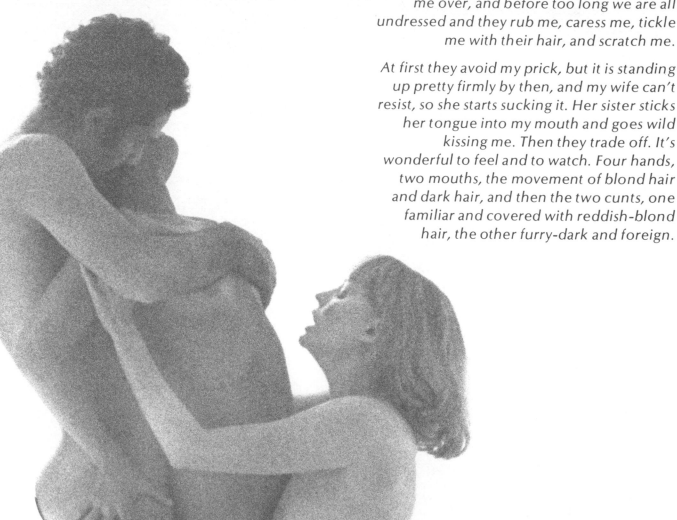

 *Strip Poker*

A fantasy? I don't know if I have any real fantasies, but I do imagine playing strip poker with my wife and some of our friends. In my imagination we go much further than we ever have in actuality. Not only do some of us end up nude, but all of us end up on the carpet in a big heap with everybody doing everything to everybody. It's a real turn-on.

I think of it sometimes when I am in bed with my wife. I wonder if she would get angry if I told her. No? You don't think so? You think she might be fantasizing, too?

Breaking the Taboo

In our sexual fantasies we often do whatever is to us most prohibited. A Catholic man might imagine making love to a nun or the Madonna herself. A religious woman might imagine making love to a rabbi or minister. Since our society prohibits incest, fantasies of being sexually involved with sister or brother, mother or father, are not uncommon. A man who is faithful to his wife and a conventional life might imagine trying everything that is possible to try in a bordello. Both women and men who are firmly heterosexual imagine homosexual encounters. Ancient taboos against bestiality are part of the reason horses, dogs, and other animals appear so frequently in sexual fantasies.

The strength of the taboo heightens its appeal. We imagine things we would never actually want to do or be able to do. In the fantasy, we try to reach ultimate freedom by breaking the taboo.

 *Kaffeeklatsch*

This is Steve's story:

My mother always had a lot of friends over, and one day I walked into the kitchen where they were having coffee, and one of them was sitting on a stool in such a way that I could see all the way up her skirt. She was sort of fat, and her thighs looked so soft. I remember wishing I could slide my hands up those thighs.

It was long ago—I couldn't have been more than fourteen —and the glimpse lasted just a second, for she readjusted herself on the stool when I came into the room. But ever since then, I sometimes imagine myself being invisible and walking into that room, sliding my hands up her thighs, just poking around and feeling her. In my fantasy the women neither see me nor feel me, so they go on talking and drinking coffee while I take my time. It still gets me excited to think about it.

THE MAN UNDER THE BED

The man under the bed
The man who has been there for years waiting
The man who waits for my floating bare foot
The man who is silent as dustballs riding the darkness
The man whose breath is the breathing of small white butterflies

The man whose breathing I hear when I pick up the phone
The man in the mirror whose breath blackens silver
The boneman in closets who rattles the mothballs
The man at the end of the end of the line

I met him tonight I always meet him
He stands in the amber air of a bar
When the shrimp curl like beckoning fingers
& ride through the air on their toothpick skewers
When the ice cracks & I am about to fall through
he arranges his face around its hollows
he opens his pupilless eyes at me
For years he has waited to drag me down
& now he tells me
he has only waited to take me home
We waltz through the street like death & the maiden
We float through the wall of the wall of my room

If he's my dream he will fold back into my body
His breath writes letters of mist on the glass of my cheeks
I wrap myself around him like the darkness
I breathe into his mouth
& make him real

ERICA JONG

Sleeping Beauty

I like to watch my daughter and her friends. Girls at her age are so seductive and feminine, and yet they are little children at the same time. Looking at them, you just know that little breasts will be popping out any day, and their hips will get wide, and they will start to fuss with clothes and hair dryers and curlers and makeup.

My daughter kisses me, of course, and I like it, and I don't think of it as erotic, but at the same time I really enjoy thinking about all the changes that are happening to her body. Even in her games she seems to change from day to day—one day she pretends she is a horse, the next day she plays dress-up and wears her mama's clothes.

As I said, I enjoy observing her and her little friends. But once, when my daughter had a friend spend the night, as she often does on weekends, I came downstairs in the morning, to see my daughter's little friend asleep in the TV room. She was almost naked. Her chest was flat, but her nipples looked as if they were swollen. She had reddish-blond hair between her legs. Her skin looked so smooth. I really wanted to touch her. But I didn't. But I do think of that little girl.

I imagine coming up to her and touching her cheek and kissing her face— very, very gently—and maybe going as far as stroking her legs and arms and maybe even her breasts. Sometimes I do imagine even kissing her body— oh, so gently. I don't really want her to wake up from her sleep. That's all I do. I think of her as Sleeping Beauty.

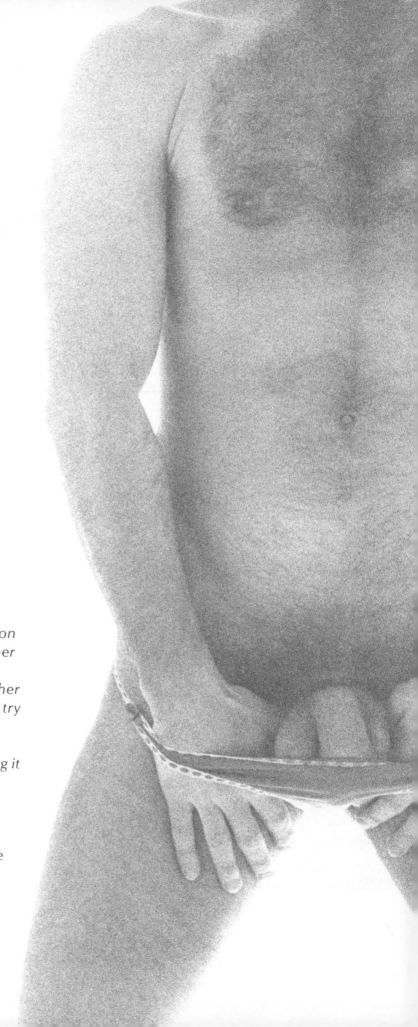

 Dressing Up

Sometimes when my wife is away, I put on her clothes. I like the smell and feel of her underthings—you know, the bra, a slip, her panties. When we make love, I like her to wear clothes, and when she is away, I try them on. I feel very naughty when I do, and it scares me that someone might discover what I do. I think I started doing it when I was fourteen, just after mother died. Maybe I was pretending I was her and still alive. I don't know. I do like clothes, and I always go along when my wife wants to add to her wardrobe. I like feminine clothes—laces and silks and scarfs. Things with ruffles and flowers.

 # The Hostess

The wife of a friend of mine is pretty much of a flirt, especially when she has had a few drinks, and once when I was at their house for dinner, she was playing footsies with me all through the meal. It isn't easy to choke on chocolate mousse, but I did.

In my daydreams I return to that dinner party. There are eight of us at the table, and suddenly I feel a foot in my lap. The foot wiggles, and I move closer to the table so no one will see what is going on. Her toes manage to find whatever she is searching for, and she moves them around my hard-on while all kinds of neat little phrases slip into her conversation.

"It's delicious to lick it slowly like that" (supposedly referring to the dessert).

"It's so nice and hard" (referring to cookies served with the dessert).

"Some like it hot" (as she offers her guests coffee).

"The bigger the better" (referring to a discussion on charity donations).

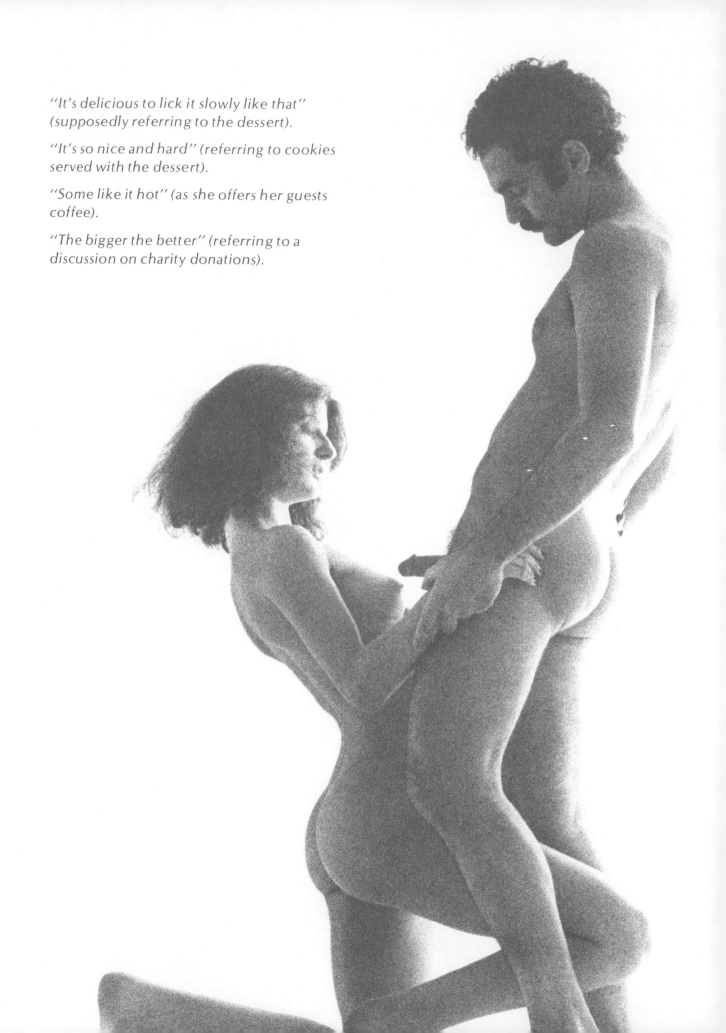

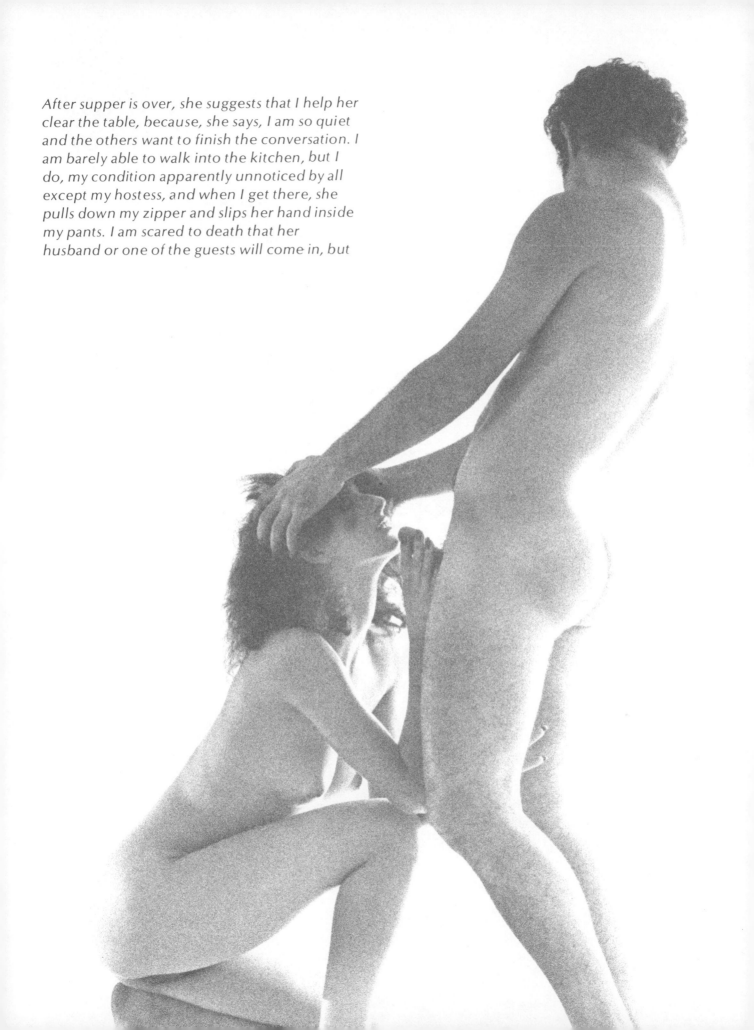

After supper is over, she suggests that I help her clear the table, because, she says, I am so quiet and the others want to finish the conversation. I am barely able to walk into the kitchen, but I do, my condition apparently unnoticed by all except my hostess, and when I get there, she pulls down my zipper and slips her hand inside my pants. I am scared to death that her husband or one of the guests will come in, but

she seems to have no fear and pulls out my cock and sucks it good, but I mean really good, in and out, her tongue circling the head, licking and sucking, until I come inside her mouth. When we are done, she says: "Nothing like a good dessert to finish off a meal."

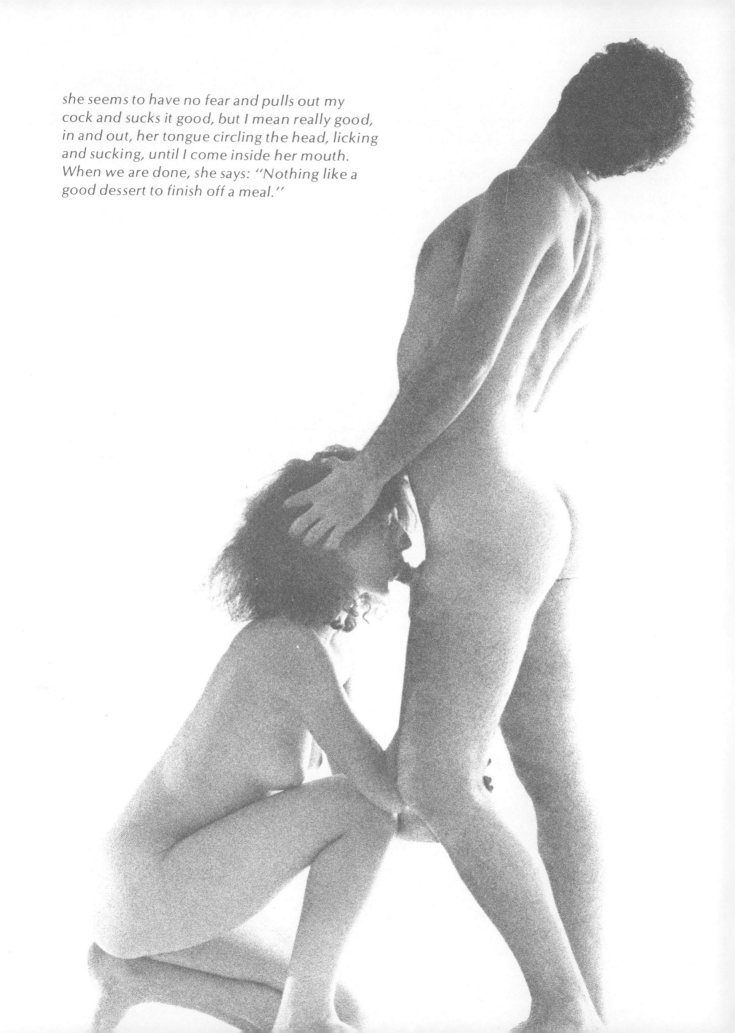

 *YOUR*
NIPPLES

sit like snaps
on your chest, tiny,

breasts being
forgotten. But they harden
to my touch.

And somewhere within you
a small cunt
sucks at empty

space. Lying near you
I sometimes wish
a small part of me

could grow, to move
inside you.

# The Teacher

I think it would be wonderfully exciting to teach a young man about sex, to show him how a woman likes to be touched, and when, and where. I sometimes think of this after a bath when I am alone and undressed. I pretend my hands are the hands of the young boy, and they start, slowly as if he were shy, by touching my face, my hair, and my neck. Then the fingers follow the shape of my lips. I open my mouth and pull a finger inside and suck it, rolling my tongue around it, then I let the wet finger explore my nipples, gently circling the areolae and tweaking and pulling at the nipples. The hands knead my breasts awhile, and I picture him sucking the nipples while a hand slides down my belly. The hands roam all over my hips and thighs, sometimes caressing, sometimes scratching gently.

In my imagination, I let him know it is all right for him to touch my cunt hairs and open these lips. I pretend he is shy and touches the strange hairs cautiously at first. I show him how to pinch the lips together and squeeze the clit inside. Then I show him how to lick his fingers and slide them down the crack and then into the cunt. While one hand rubs and tweaks the clit indirectly, the other slips in and out of me. When I start to get really hot, I

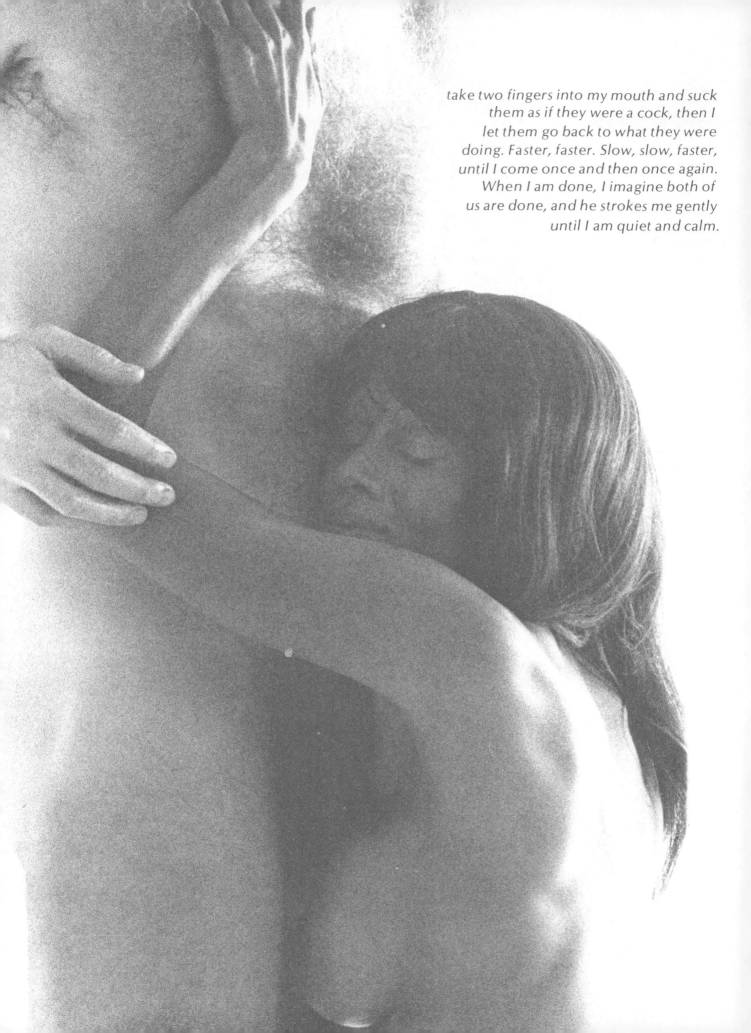

take two fingers into my mouth and suck them as if they were a cock, then I let them go back to what they were doing. Faster, faster. Slow, slow, faster, until I come once and then once again. When I am done, I imagine both of us are done, and he strokes me gently until I am quiet and calm.

 # Mary Contrary

I used to be very religious when I was younger, and I was very proud of myself when I was old enough to go to confession. I liked the whole mystery of the church—prayers, candlelight, embroideries, wafers, and wine. And I liked the secrecy of the confession booth. I guess I was going through a lot of teenage crushes in those days and felt the usual mixture of delight and guilt, and it seemed both strange and exciting to talk to the priest about them. I couldn't see him, but I could hear him, and I knew he was there behind the curtain

I knew about the things I shouldn't do, and I knew that the church had the ability to condone and forgive; and somehow the two ideas started to mix in my mind, and I began to imagine the priest touching me where I should not let anyone touch me. The secrecy of the confessional became the secrecy of my imagination, and behind this curtain the priest and I could do all kinds of things.

That was a long time ago, and I understand these things better now. But I still think the dark-red and purple curtains used in church are erotic somehow.

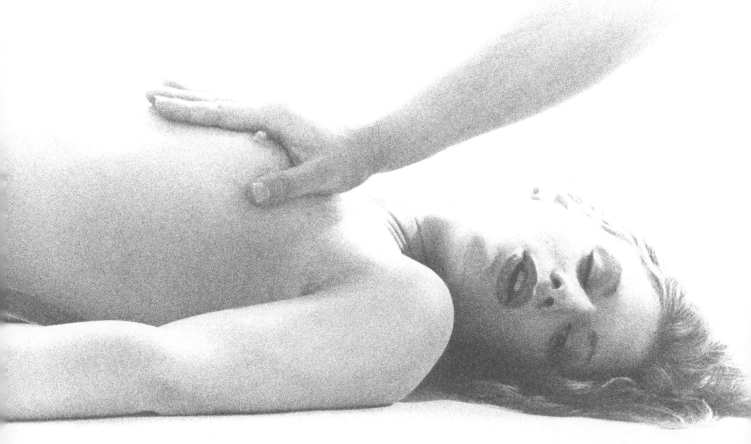

# Being Godlike

If we look into almost any religion or mythology, we will find stories about humans who copulate with animals. In the supernatural realms that are described in ancient texts, gods frolic with birds, cattle, and mythical beasts.

The stories about Zeus and his disguises are numerous. In the shape of a swan, he made love to Leda. In the shape of a bull, he carried the lovely maiden Europa away. Somebody made up those stories once upon a time, and the contemporary imagination can be equally full of fanciful beasts. Though actual bestiality is uncommon, fantasies about bestiality are not unusual.

 *Deer Me*

I go deer hunting every fall, but I must admit I do it more for the sake of getting out in the woods than for the sake of hunting. I haven't killed a deer in years. A few ducks and grouse, yes, but not deer.

I think I stopped hunting for the sake of killing one fall when I saw the most beautiful doe standing in a clearing. I was walking, and she surprised me by just standing there, even though she heard me. She just stood still, looking

at me. There was something so vulnerable in those large brown eyes and something so feminine about her whole being that I could only think of holding her, protecting her, and loving her. Ever since that time, I occasionally think about fucking deer—you know, being the buck and fucking in a thicket, fucking a doe like that—you know, really being part of the forest.

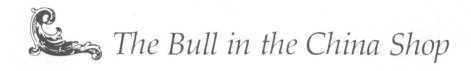

The Bull in the China Shop

You know that phrase "A bull in a china shop"? I remember wondering about its meaning when I was a boy, and I still think about it; that is, I picture myself as the bull.

I imagine going into a store full of delicate things like glassware, jewelry, flowers, or Christmas ornaments. The saleslady is pretty and alone—you know, one of those cool-looking, pseudosophisticated dames? Yeah, and I start chasing her. I grab for her, and a table gets knocked over; I almost catch her, and a display case breaks. I get hold of her arm, and some dainty objects crash to the floor.

When I finally catch her, I go through similar acts of knocking her down, pulling off her blouse, tearing off her pants, and as I finally get her pinned and I enter her, I hear the police sirens. Eeeee-ooooo-eeeee-ooooo. What a climax! And of course I always have time to finish and escape before the cops arrive on the scene.

 ## Man's Best Friend

When I was a little girl we had a dog, and the dog was in heat, and, as you can imagine, this attracted the neighborhood males. My mother told me not to watch "the stupid animals," but I was fascinated by what they were doing. I will never forget seeing that long pink thing sticking out of the neighbor's beagle, and I couldn't help wondering how it would feel to be a stupid animal and have such a long pink thing entering me.

Sometimes when I was in bed, I would put a finger between my legs, and I would feel all warm down there as I thought about the long pink thing. Even now that I am grown and have a lover, I sometimes think about the long pink thing. I think of it when I am alone, and I sometimes think of it moving in and out of me as my lover moves in and out of me from behind.

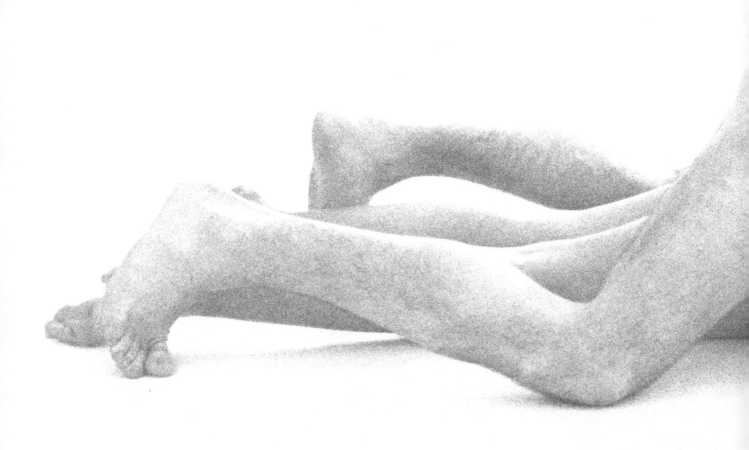

Would a Rose?

A rose by any other name might smell as sweet, but the words used to describe sexual acts or parts can make a difference to both the speaker and the listener.

It is important for each person to try to find out how he or she reacts to different words, and, if possible, why. If the phrase *making love* is the one you are used to using, try using *fuck* and see how you react. The word *fuck* might seem risquè to you and therefore more erotic, or it might sound dirty to you and therefore turn you off. If you are used to saying *fuck*, try using *making love*. The latter might let the emotion of love enter into an act you keep at a distance by thinking of it as being merely physical, or *making love* might seem tame and romantic to you and therefore unexciting.

Everyone has preferences, and it is possible that one's scope of action and reaction can change by a change of the language.

I like the hard sounds of the words *fuck, lick, suck, cunt,* and *cock.* Interesting, isn't it, how many sexual words use the "k" sound? Notice *dick, prick, sex, box, clit.* Then there are *butt, boob, belly, breasts, buns, balls.* The alliteration is amazing—maybe I am making a sound poem? *Tits, tail, pussy, snatch, butch, bush, babe, bang, button.* How do you like the words *dude, dong, fag, gay, cubes, mother-fucker?* I think the word *intercourse* sounds a bit formal in conversation, but I like the words *fellatio* and *cunnilingus*—they sound delicious to me. What about you? Do you know which words turn your lover on?

You might like words that upset your lover, or vice versa. It is wise to be sensitive to the fact that people are bothered by some words and aroused by others. Your father might be shocked by the words you use, your daughter might be surprised, and your lover might be excited. Since it is best to know what the situation is, a little verbal experimentation could be constructive.

Language patterns and word usage change all the time, and it is interesting to note how certain words are expected and accepted from certain groups, while they are shocking

from other groups. Though a man at a cocktail party might tell jokes and talk about a fuck or who is screwing whom, etc., he might be shocked if his mother started a sentence with: "My fucking neighbors . . ."

To use a less controversial example, it might seem right if a group of teenagers or college kids used expressions like *with it, uptight, rap, rip off, off the wall, gross,* and *let it all hang out,* but it might seem odd and "phony" if a sixty-year-old businessman did the same. It is not a bad idea to question why we categorize people and put language fences around them. Is there a language for the bar? For the church? For poker with the boys? For lunch with the girls? For bed? For children? For husband? For lover?

Words are not simple and naked. Each one comes complete with a certain amount of emotional baggage. A word has a sound and a sensual makeup

that consists of its various meanings, connotations, and, in addition to all this, whatever emotional value the speaker attributes to it *and* the emotional value the listener attributes to it. This can make a word almost as powerful as a bomb, and a person who has his language under control is virtually the owner of a power plant.

The belief that words have power is as ancient as any written document we know. *In the beginning was the word, and the word was God.* Verbal and written spells exist all over the world, and they are based on the belief that the word itself is magical. It was once believed that something could be contained in its name. Evil could be warded off with the right incantation. The power of a prayer or a spell could be strengthened by adding words like *Father, Son,* and *Holy Ghost* or any of a variety of words referring to sexual parts. If a woman said a spell or a curse using sexual words, that spell was believed to have yet additional power.

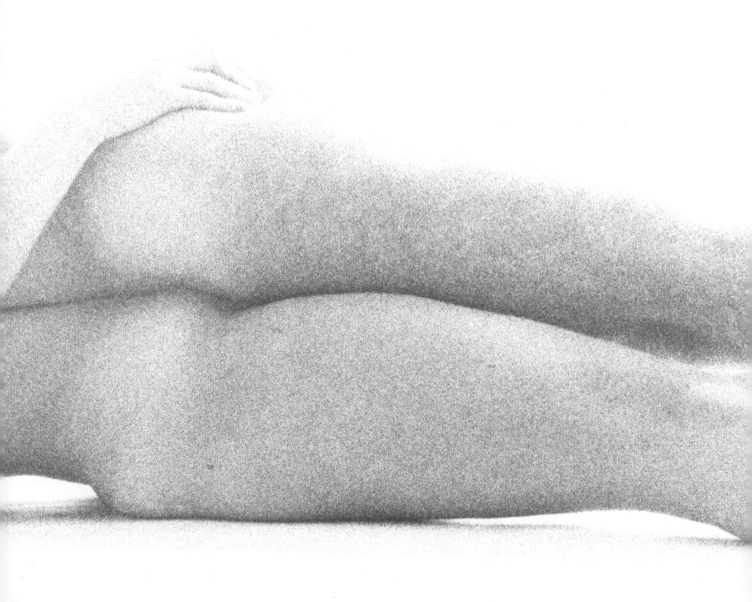

As an example, here is an
ancient spell from Sweden. It was
said in the evening when the embers
were covered with ashes so that
the fire would remain aglow
through the night.

 FIRE PRAYER

Ashy, Ballbox,
Cunt, Tattlemouse,
This fire shall never
Go out in my house.

MONOSYLLABLE POEM

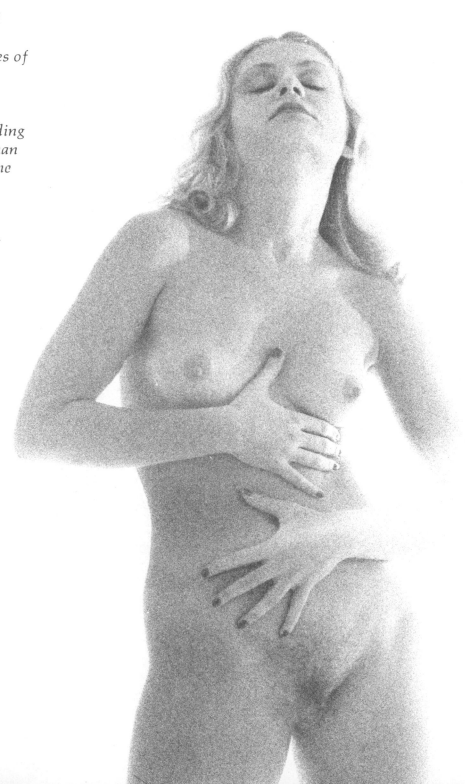

nathaniel
named it baby hole, i
the poet fall back
lamely on cunt and snatch,
pussy and twat. holy mother
in farmer and henley's
dictionary of slang and
its analogues there are
eight and one half pages of
small type to say what
i am trying to say and
that was victorian
england. under its heading
of monosyllable whitman
said bath of birth, donne
said best-worst part,
herrick the bower of
bliss, sterne the
covered way, rochester
the crown of sense but

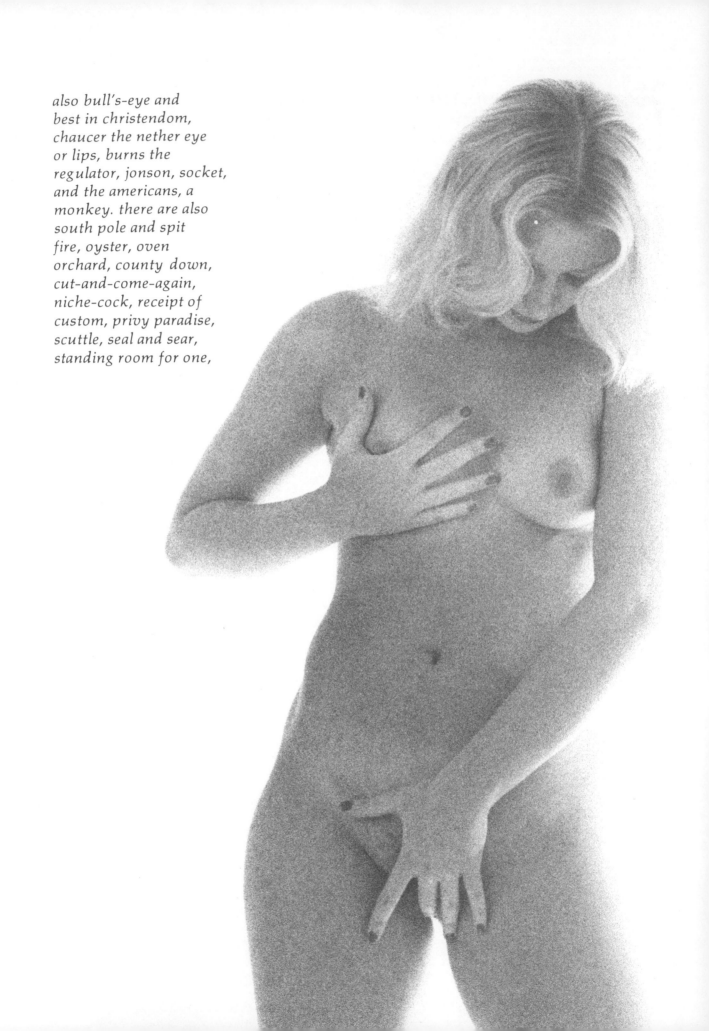

also bull's-eye and
best in christendom,
chaucer the nether eye
or lips, burns the
regulator, jonson, socket,
and the americans, a
monkey. there are also
south pole and spit
fire, oyster, oven
orchard, county down,
cut-and-come-again,
niche-cock, receipt of
custom, privy paradise,
scuttle, seal and sear,
standing room for one,

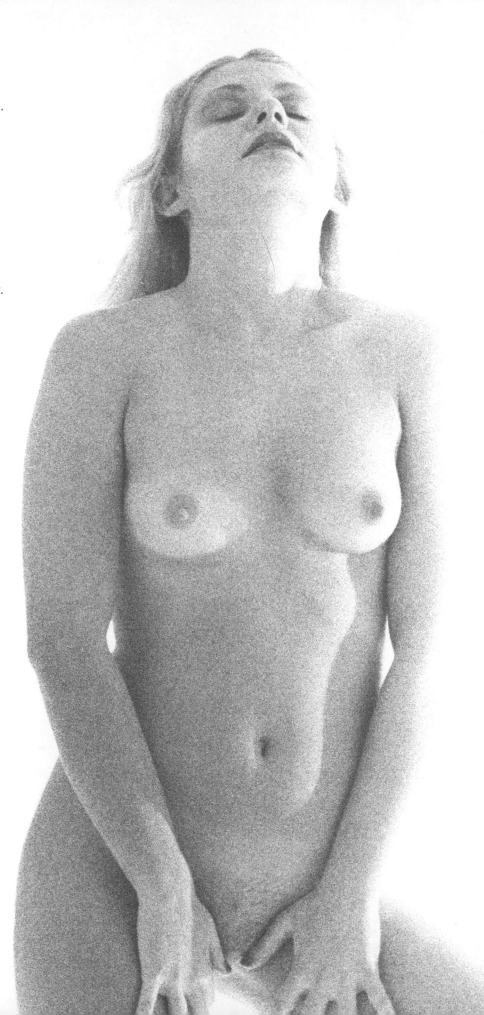

sugar basin, thatched
house, upright wink . . .
holy mother we are so
afraid that there are no
words. she was sitting
legs open and i saw the
warm fur and wanted
into it holy mother—
as the spanish say
of it it is the
madre soledad, lonely
mother. i wanted into it.

JOEL OPPENHEIMER

 # The Fairy Tale

Are you too old for fairy tales? Let's look at a basic story line of a classic fairy tale.

A little boy who is walking in the forest meets a big, ugly troll. The boy has heard about trolls and is afraid that this big, ugly troll will eat him up. The troll might try to befriend the boy by saying: "Come with me into my cave, and I will give you a pot of gold." The boy would like the pot of gold, but he is very scared of the troll. He might even remember being warned about the monsters that inhabit the dark forest. But he does want the pot of gold.

The troll falls asleep by the cave, and the boy decides to take advantage of the sleeping troll and go into the cave and find the pot of gold. Although he is scared, the boy enters the cave. He walks through the narrow entrance and is amazed to see that the inside of the cave is a large and beautiful room. All kinds of wonders can be found there: delicious foods, jewels, magical animals, strange music.

The boy is so overwhelmed with the riches of the cave that he almost forgets his fear, but then he hears the troll stir. He starts to run out of the cave, but it is too late. The troll wakes up and confronts him. He expects the troll to be angry, perhaps to crush him, or to eat him up. But the troll touches him gently and says: "I have always wanted to meet someone who is brave. As a reward for your bravery, let me give you my pot of gold."

The young man who for the first time comes face-to-face with a cunt might be as scared as the little boy who meets the troll. Genitals might seem demanding of a lover, just as if they were saying: "Please me, or else!" Men sometimes know the ancient and universal fear of being swallowed by that cave. A vagina accepts the large, erect penis and gives it back small and limp. It can take a seed that is so small that we can't see it without a microscope, and change this seed into a whole child. The very act of creation happens behind the magical doors of the vulva. It is familiar with transformations. The vagina can be dry or moist. It can change from large to small to large and back again, many times during sexual play. In various cultures in different parts of the world, there are stories that say that women used to have teeth inside their vaginas. The concept is referred to as *vagina dentata*. Men were actually so scared of being "eaten up" that the vagina was depicted with teeth.

Fairy tales do not need to be interpreted—they can simply be enjoyed—but let me play with the similarity I have presented. The young man who lets his desires overcome his fear of the troll and her cave finds himself in a wondrous world. He enjoys being in the cave. Not only does he like being there, but to his surprise he is given its riches. He does not have to steal the pleasure of being there. He is given additional pleasures.

🐍 VAGINA DENTATA

Bite by bite
you undo the love-me-love-me-not
daisy of the egg, sunny-side-up,
you cooked for my Sunday
breakfast.

And the fast we break
*   is the one we broke*
When my egg splattered its red morning
and you said "You taste of strange
metals" and you were the alchemist
using heat to make
gold.

*   "Bite me back" you said*
and I do, though I don't need teeth.
I give you the old woman you like.
She is toothless, wise. She sucks
her food.

Since the previous story deals with a young man meeting his monster, let's look at the classic frog-turning-into-a-prince story.

A princess walks in the woods. She sees an ugly toad. You can imagine its pleading eyes. It must be terribly difficult for a delicate little princess to kiss an ugly toad. But she does. And, as we already know, the ugly toad is miraculously transformed into a handsome prince. In some versions of the story they marry and live happily ever after.

Now we can, of course, leave the story as story, but stories very often have a tie to reality. In my world there are very few real princesses and even fewer ones who actually kiss real frogs. But in the world I know, there are many young women who confront the metaphorical frog of a man's genitals. The different textures of skin on testicles and penis might seem strange. She might be repulsed and reluctant to touch them or kiss them.

A woman might be feared because her reproductive organs are hidden and therefore mysterious. A man might be feared because his organs are completely external. The erect penis might by its very nature seem violent. It wants to enter, it wants to intrude, and some are scared of that intrusion. The woman who overcomes her fear of male genitalia might see the penis become as handsome and appealing as any prince. If she braves her fear, her kiss is rewarded.

The fairy tale, like other fantasy, is a place where you can do extraordinary feats, be brave and strong. Anything is possible in the story. You can move from poverty to riches. You can be frog and prince, princess and troll.

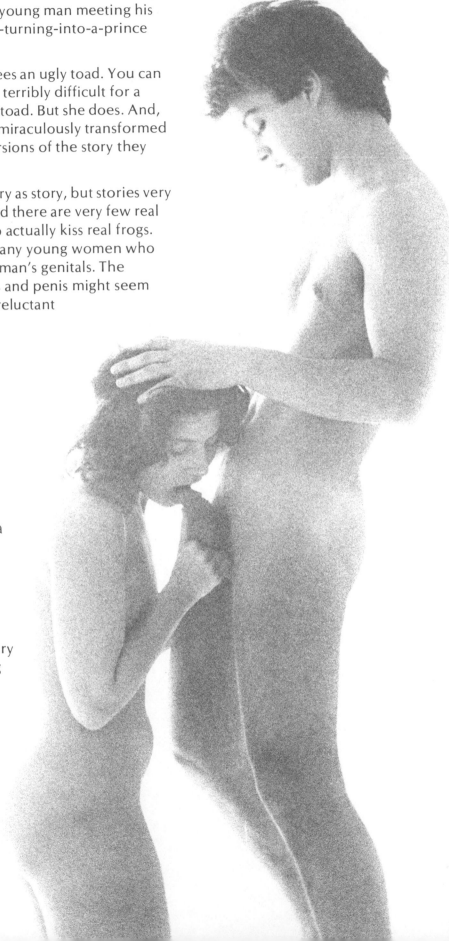

# The Emperor's New Clothes

I really like to look at women, and when I see them passing on the street, sitting in a restaurant, or dancing at a nightclub or a party, I imagine them in various states of undress. If I see a woman in a

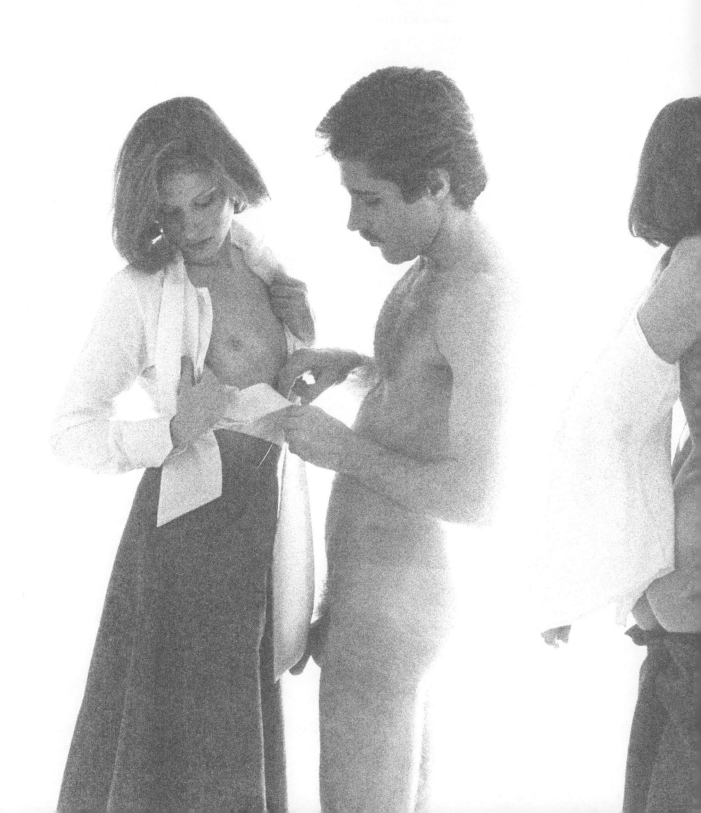

low-cut blouse, I imagine myself unbuttoning the blouse, and I visualize her slip and bra. If I see a girl in a tight skirt or jeans, it is easy to picture her hips and butt naked. Sometimes I imagine myself actually unzipping the zipper of jeans or skirt, unbuttoning the blouse, and unhooking the bra. Do I touch her? No, not really. I just like her to be naked so I can watch her.

 # "The Bogeyman"

Even after I got married I was afraid of "the bogeyman." I imagined him waiting in a closet, hiding under the bed, or lurking by the cellar stairs. Though I knew better, I sometimes hesitated to go into the basement or to open a closet that long had been closed. I did not keep my fear secret. Sometimes I pouted playfully and said to my husband: "I'm afraid of the bogeyman."

One day when I did that, my husband said: "Oh, it's just your own sexuality that you are afraid of."

There it was, out in the open. What he said rang so true that I could not deny it, even to myself. I understood that there was something in me that was both scared and desirous of some unnamed man lurking in the dark. Did I want him to come and grab me and take me into his closet or basement? This new look at my childish fantasies erased the fear.

Most adults do not read fairy tales, at least not for their own enjoyment. But most adults do go to the movies, and the movie world is a place where we can confront the hero and the monster. You have probably seen movies about the bad crook who wins out in the end and the prostitute who comes to the rescue. Poor becomes rich, and rich becomes poor. In movies we beat the system, we have secret love affairs, we win the chase, and we kiss the star. No one could count how many women have kissed Robert Redford in their daydreams. And Marilyn Monroe has entered many a man's imaginary bed. The fairy tales continue, and we enter them. We test our loves and fears and hopes as we identify with the characters on the screen. We carry the movie image or story in our minds and relive it. *Movie, fantasy, story, fairy tale, daydream, memory, hope*—the words are almost interchangeable. The ordinary mixes with the extraordinary. Reality and dream are compatible partners in the mind.

Have you ever played tiger?

Have you ever played horse and
tossed your mane, neighing?

Have you ever said that your penis is a mole who must get to know his lover? Have you taken it in your hand and let it explore a back, thighs, hands, the space under the chin, an armpit, a navel? Have you let it circle nipples, poke into a vagina, and let it end its blind exploration in the dark hole of a rectum?

Have you let your arms become
snakes slithering around you both
as you make love?

Have you played together,
rolling and tumbling across
the floor?

Arabian Nights

I like to pretend that I have a harem where I reign supreme. A hundred gorgeous girls in all shapes and sizes cater to my every whim. They are wives and slaves, maids and mistresses and prostitutes. Sometimes I am aggressive, beat them, and make all kinds of demands. Sometimes I lie passive and let them take the lead.

As a Man Thinketh . . .

To a man, his penis is the symbol of his maleness, and that maleness is very often synonymous with *power*. A man who thinks his organ is not as big as it could or should be might think himself into all kinds of complexes. The truth of the matter is that vaginal contact has very little to do with female orgasm, and though most women do want to be

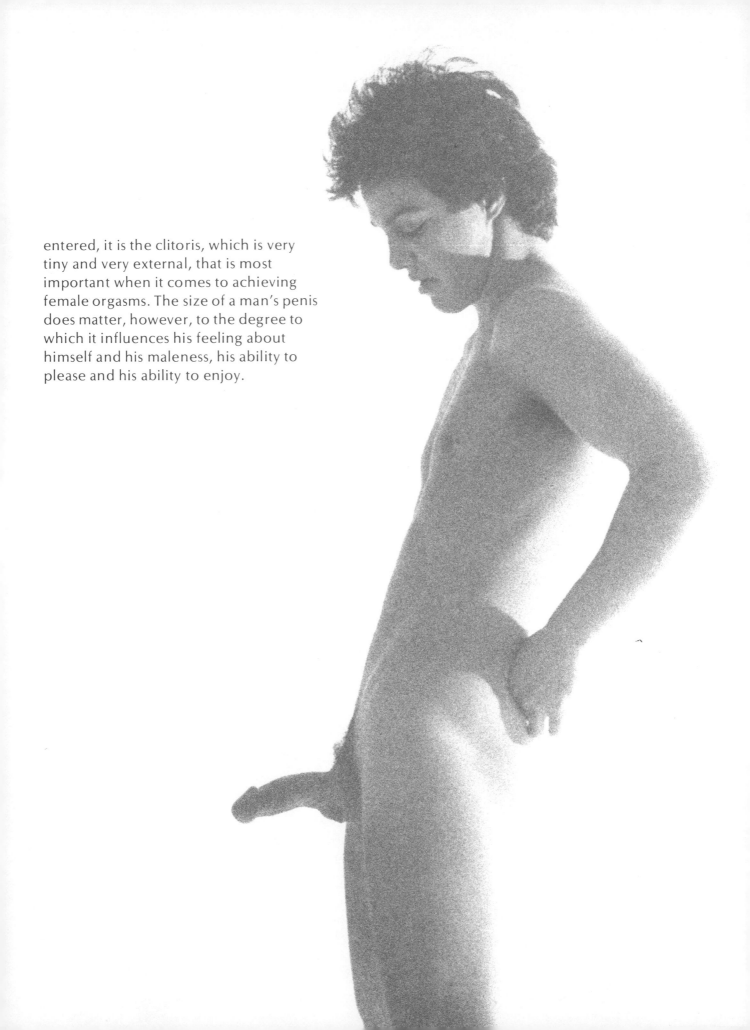

entered, it is the clitoris, which is very tiny and very external, that is most important when it comes to achieving female orgasms. The size of a man's penis does matter, however, to the degree to which it influences his feeling about himself and his maleness, his ability to please and his ability to enjoy.

The More the Merrier

Like lots of guys, I often wake up with a hard-on; so, instead of getting right up and into the shower, I lie there, halfway awake, and imagine that I am away someplace and asleep, and two, three girls are trying to wake me. They tug at me, call me "sir," pull at my covers, and then they start to touch me. I picture a place like Tahiti or Samoa. When the girls see my big cock, they start to play. They look young and act young, but their hands are all over me and so quick and skillful on my prick that I explode.

The Supermarket

One night I had the funniest dream. I was walking up and down the aisles of a supermarket, and there, on one of the shelves, was an assortment of penises. They were of all sizes and shapes, circumsised and uncircumsised, and each was labeled according to brand, and priced. It was wonderful. I stood a long time in front of the display before I made my selection. I was very conscious of the thought of getting just the right one for that particular week, and aware of the fact that I would certainly try other shapes and sizes at other times.

It was such a funny dream, and every time I remember it I smile. Now, I sometimes daydream about such a supermarket, or sometimes when I see men riding buses or walking streets I wonder what kind of supermarket samples they are carrying in their pants.

 *Erotic Pictures*

Erotic pictures have been used for both pleasure and education for ages. They have been used as guides toward spiritual fulfillment, as history lessons, and as sexual stimulation.

Prehistoric pictures of men with overgrown penises were chiseled into rocks in Scandinavia. In Indian temples one can see, carved in stone, figures that depict all kinds of sexual union: couples having intercourse in every possible position, scenes showing group sex and bestiality. Erotic paintings can be seen on the walls in Pompeii. The Phallus of Heaven was carried in Shinto religious processions in Japan, as well as in Dionysian cults.

The lines between art and pornography keep changing. It wasn't long ago that the so-called French postcard, or dirty picture, was secretively bought and sold. The present-day pornographic movie and magazine still have a dubious reputation. On a recent visit to Pompeii, I found that one of the most famous paintings is kept under lock and key. The Italian guard lets one know it can be seen. Local visitors who are female usually walk away, and the men and foreign women can watch the guard unlock a door built especially to cover this one painting. When the door is open, one can see a wonderfully amusing picture of a man weighing his enormous penis on a tiny scale.

Though once accepted art is now, by some, labeled pornographic, things that were taboo are no longer so. It was only a few years ago that pubic hair was not allowed to be shown in major American magazines. Contemporary artists such as Warhol, Wesselman, Oldenburg, Moore,

and Rivers deal openly, and delightfully, with erotic imagery. Other artists who have done exemplary erotic art include Michelangelo, Leonardo da Vinci, Rodin, Turner, Picasso, and Brancusi.

One can only speculate about the reasons behind the early cave drawings in Africa, France, or Scandinavia. Some were probably meant to tell a story, some were meant to chronicle historic deeds, some were done as charms to guarantee a successful hunt, and some might have been done for the pleasure of executing the art and having something to see.

The Hindu religion makes it clear that sexuality is a divine part of creation. Couples making love in every possible way adorn the temples in India, and most temples have a phallic icon as the center of worship. The latter is a sacred symbol of the seminal energy that flows through the universe. Female genitalia, called yoni, are often depicted combined with the male symbol, lingam. For good luck, temple visitors will often lick a finger and touch the yoni of a sculpture near the gate. Not only is the sexual act sanctified, to Hindu thinking, but it is supposed to be a step toward enlightenment. It is believed that erotic pleasures help in transcending the world of the senses, and the statues are meant to stimulate the pilgrims.

In Chinese culture and art, we learn that a combination of yin and yang, the female and male elements, lies at the root of all being and gives life to all things. The I Ching, the old book of Chinese divination, is based upon the idea of union between the male and the female: black and white, heaven and earth, male and female genitals. In Chinese art, clouds and rain symbolize sexual intercourse between heaven and earth, and the much-valued jade is supposedly the petrified semen of the celestial dragon. A woman who does fellatio is said to "play on the flute of jade."

In the Orient there has been an unbroken tradition of art that was used as erotic encouragement. "Bride's scrolls" and "position pictures" were handed down from mother to daughter, often given to the young woman at the time of her engagement to marry. Scrolls of erotic prints, called "pillow books," were kept in pillow boxes, easily available for visual stimulation.

In Japan the making and use of erotic prints was completely accepted, and all masters of Japanese art spent a good part of their time exploring the erotic image. The idea behind it was simply that one of the greatest possible pleasures is that of sexual union. The books were meant to stimulate erotic thought and action. In Japanese art, it was very common to exaggerate the size of the genitals.

 # *Breasts*

It wouldn't be fair to talk about the size of the penis
without talking about the size of breasts. Here again, there
are small ones and large ones, soft ones and hard ones,
those with tiny brown nipples and those with large pink
ones. And for each type and size there is surely someone
who daydreams about just that shape and size.

Did you know that in South America there was a
goddess who had four hundred breasts? Fertility goddesses
of old were often depicted with many breasts, and in
Frascati, Italy, breads in the shapes of women with more
than two breasts are still baked and eaten at a certain
religious festival. Not only the ancients were fascinated
by breasts; our culture pays a lot of attention to the bust
line, fashions that emphasize the breasts, padded bras,
ways of improving their size, and directions on how to
play with them and please them.

This is a story out of Greek mythology. Zeus had been
philandering, as usual, and one of his mistresses had given
birth to a child. Since the child was born to a mortal,
it was mortal, and Zeus wanted the child to be immortal.
He brought it to Hera, who was asleep, and lay the child
down beside her. The idea was that the child would suckle
milk from Hera's breasts and thus receive immortality.
But Hera woke up, and, seeing what Zeus had done, she
turned away from the child. The drops of milk that
squirted from her breasts created the stars in the heavens
and the plants on earth.

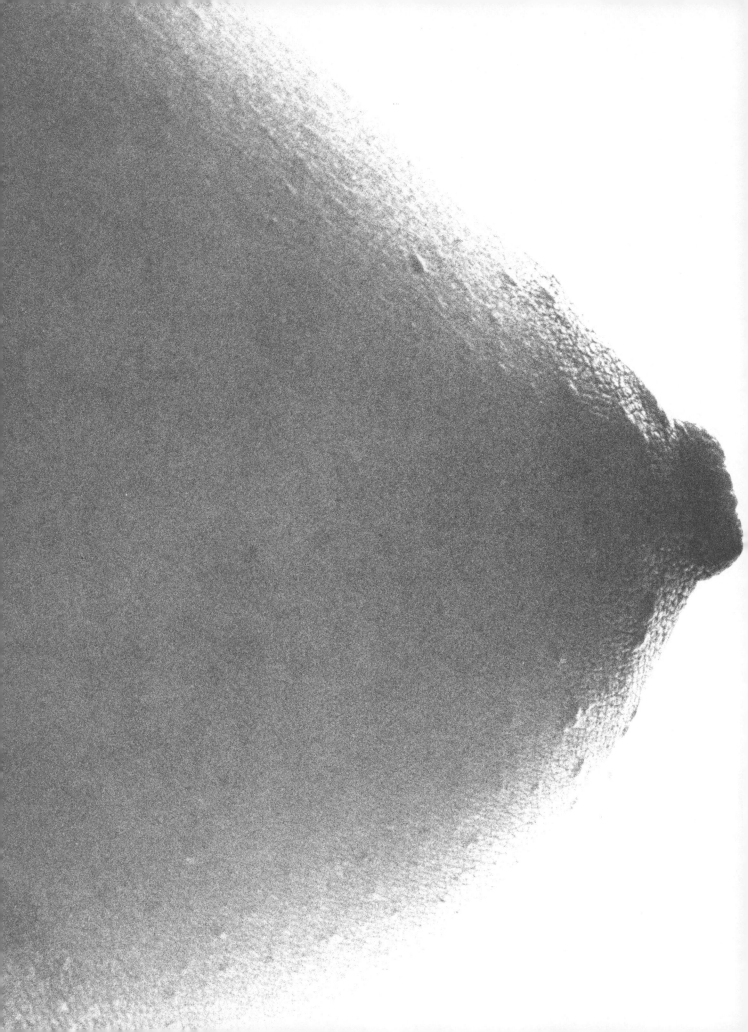

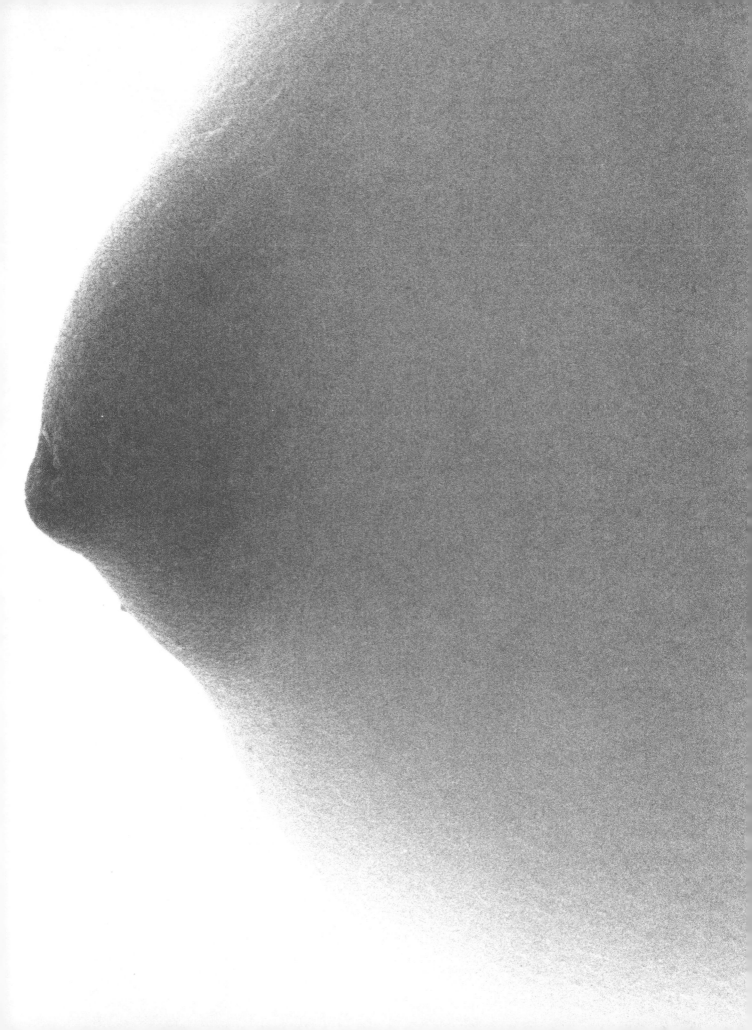

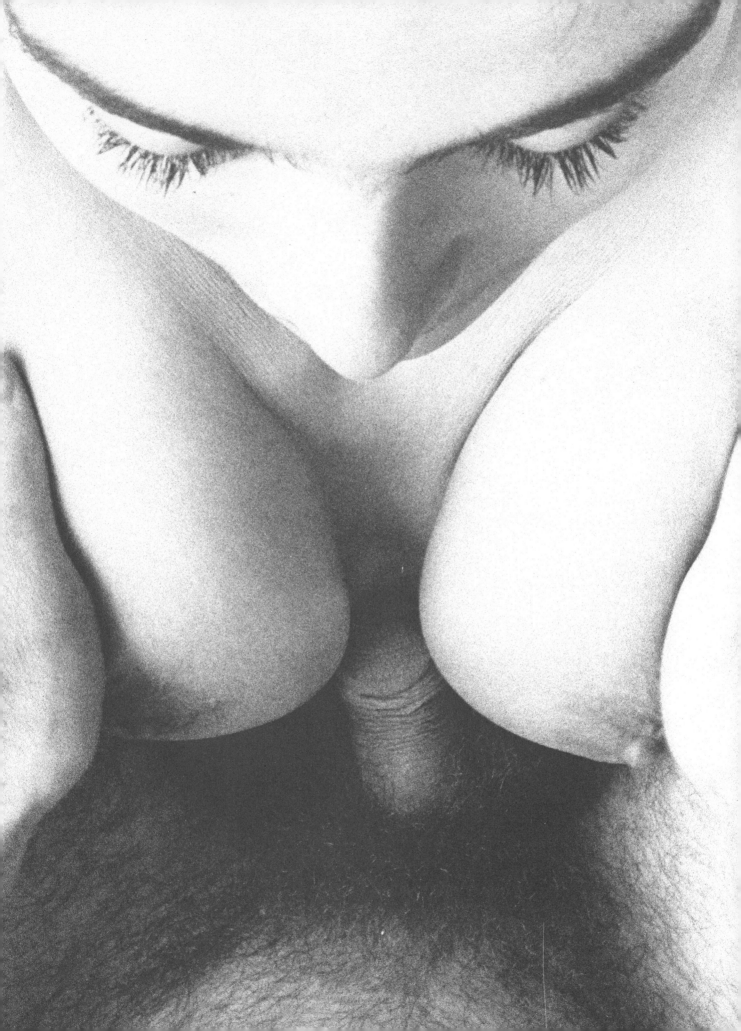

 # Booby Trap

I really do think I have a fixation. I just love breasts. I know it is impossible, but I want to be enveloped, engulfed, covered, surrounded by breasts. I dream of someone brushing my back with nipples. Once, a big-breasted woman said her breasts were the perfect murder weapon. She said she could smother someone with her breasts and there would be no sign of a clue. I would love to be smothered by breasts. I imagine two large breasts wrapped around my penis. Breasts. Breasts. Any kind of breasts.

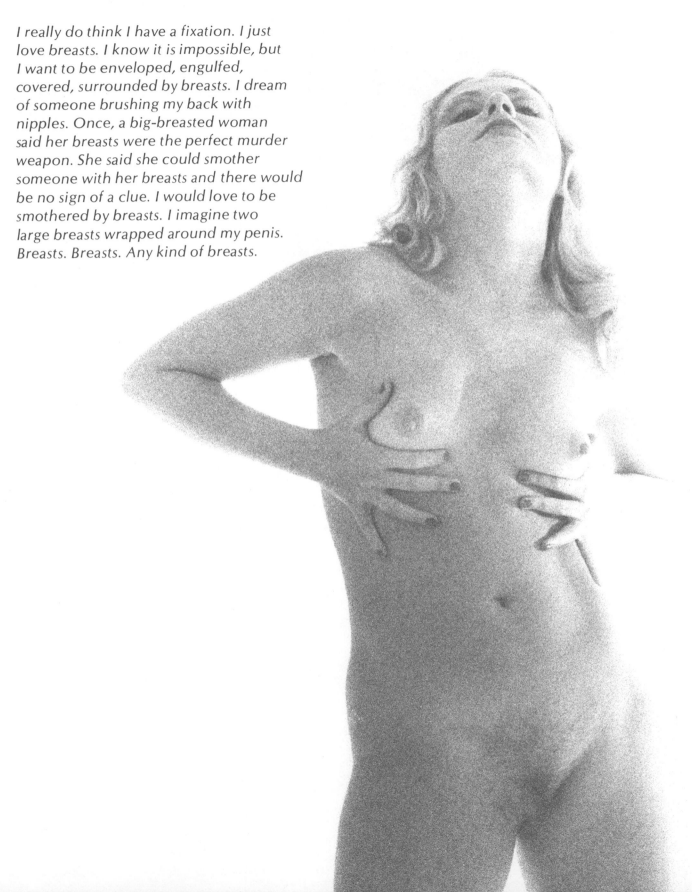

 *BREASTS*

There is something between us.

DONALD HALL

YOUR
TITS POEM

your tits have become
a barometer of our
life which i check
constantly for readings,
storm warnings, hints
of cooling rain or
the mistral rising in
the south. tornadoes
come and hurricanes
and calm fair days
and ice. they pillow
between us sometimes
when we embrace
standing or lying down.
they look smaller
in your clothes than
when nakedly exposed.
you bend to do
something and they
swing like dugs. that
also excites me. you
used to sit above me
and they brushed my
chest as they swung.
you used to take my hand
as it held your
nipple, you used
to take your nipple
yourself. you once
came to orgasm
with the rolling of
your nipple between my
thumb and forefinger,
steadily, slowly.

JOEL OPPENHEIMER

 # Samson or Not

Remember the story of Samson? He lost his strength when his hair was cut. Naked, we are dressed in our skin and our hair, and both can be subject to change in national, personal, professional, and religious fashion.

Remember the military's compulsory crew cut? Some religions believe the men should have long beards and long sideburns. Some believe priests and monks should be clean shaven. Some believe woman should show their hair only to their husbands. Some believe women should shave their heads when they marry.

Some cultures consider a full beard a sign of maturity and wisdom, and let their men wear it only after the age of thirty; before that, a mustache can be worn. Other cultures feel beards are symbolic

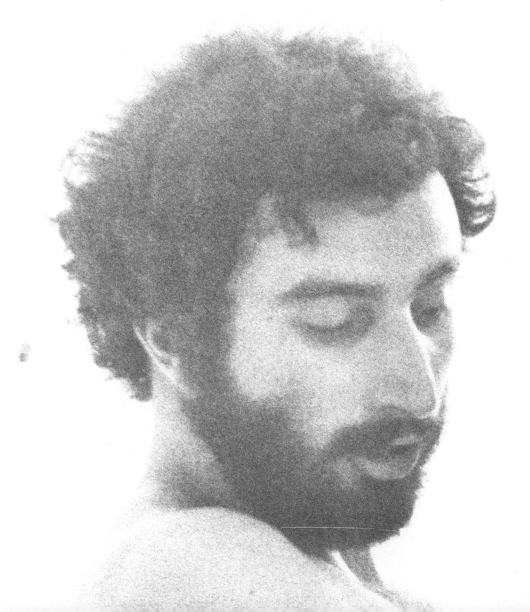

of a man's place in society, and hence only the rich and powerful are allowed to wear them. For years there was a tax on beards in Russia. The Romans went through times when all men wore beards; then no men wore beards. At times the slave owner wore a beard, but the slave had to be clean shaven. Once upon a time, mustaches were used in war in order to scare the enemy, and it was not long ago that military men were supposed to wear mustaches. In Spain, losing a mustache was like losing one's honor.

And what about a woman's hair? The fashions are as varied and amusing. One year it should be curled; the next year it should be straight. Many carry around the image of a grandmother figure who would slowly unwind her long gray hair at night. To some, long hair is a sign of femininity, to some a sign of youth, to others it seems old-fashioned.

There is fashion to hair in the armpit and the pubic region, too. A lot of women shave their armpits, and some men think that is sexy, while others are aroused at the sight of a little tuft. There are women who shave their pubic hair, and some men prefer the hairless look of little girls. Some shape the outline of the hair on the pubis to be perfectly triangular, diamond-shaped, or heart-shaped.

I asked a young girl why she was letting her hair grow. She said: "I love the way it feels on my shoulder." A woman said: "When I walk naked, my long hair touches my butt, and I like that, and there are so many things I can do with it when I make love." "What?" "Well, I can wrap it around

Steve's penis, or rub his back with it, or I can sit beside him, or on top of him, and let it caress him all over. I can cover us both with it like a blanket. He says he loves the way it whispers over him.''

Eyelashes can be used to tickle and arouse, too; this is called butterfly-kissing. And hair in any place can be tugged and held onto. What do women prefer? That depends on the woman. One told me: ''I think I like him because of his beard. That little pink mouth in the middle of all that hair—it's like a woman's cunt. It is so sexy.'' Another woman said: ''Mustaches and beards? No. The only mustache I like to see on my man is the one he gets when he is licking me.''

 *MUSTACHE*

I was thinking of
it this
morning, those
marvelous hairs that
curl around your words

and how they smelled with
frost all over
in the mountains

And yes especially of that
time on the floor
looking like the
middle part of a thick
leggy bug I could

just see
above my belly

LYN LIFSHIN

When I was away and called home, Charlie told me everything was fine, but he was having trouble staying away from kissing the kids or his mother, who was baby-sitting while I was gone. I couldn't imagine why he would want to keep from kissing them—you know, we are a very affectionate family. He said: "I haven't washed my mustache for three days and three nights because it carries the smell of your cunt in its hairs. Mmmm. I love it. And I wouldn't want mama or the kids to get a whiff of that."

Our hairy places are not the only ones subject to fashion or personal likes and dislikes. The skin is that enormously sensitive area that covers almost all of us. The feel of it can be exquisite, and to some the looks of it

matters just as much. Some like it black, some suntanned, some pale white. There are those who fall in love with freckles or a mole.

And when we get to the subject of tatoos, we enter a world of mysteries. A tattoo can represent a sailor's dream: a ship, a fish, a woman, and the words *home* and *mother*. A tattoo can be a secret message for someone special, a person's name, a private symbol on the buttocks or a breast. To some people it is repulsive, to some it is an act against God, to some it is symbolic of bravery and beauty. Some religions prohibit it, some demand it as part of tribal initiation rites. The subject is almost as unending as that of hair fashion.

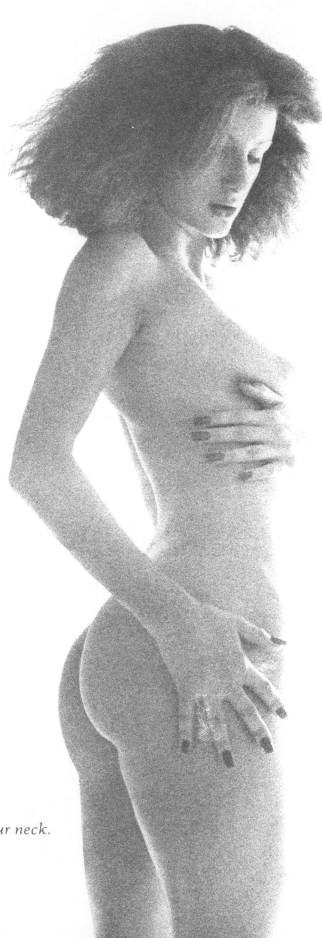

TATTOOED

When my body did not seem enough,
I had a nipple etched into each heel,
and on my buttocks, two large eyes to stare
observant of a world they had to see and feel.
A thousand hands were patterned on my thighs
to hold your body tight
and guarantee we'd never tire
our crazy rocking through the night.
My belly was a blue and swirling sea
of faces, serpents, basilisks, and birds
so that your lips, when touching me,
could touch all creatures of the world.
The moon rose on my shoulder, just for you.
The sun set in the small of my back.
My breasts were gardens, and when you left,
the dragons on my arms woke up and broke your neck.

 # Trademark

I like to imagine that I am walking on the wharf in some foreign city, and I meet a man who is tall and speaks with a foreign accent. He is a sailor on a large ship that is anchored nearby, and he asks me if I want to see his ship. I do, and we climb aboard, and he shows me everything from the lifeboat to the bridge to the engine room. He invites me for a drink, I accept, and we go to his cabin. He locks the door and gives a strange laugh and pulls off his shirt. His body is covered with tattoos.

I tell him I should be leaving, but he says No. I try to unlock the door, but he pushes me away and tells me to undress. When I refuse, he slaps my face. I undress, and when I'm done, he takes my hands, ties them together with a sash, and fastens the sash to a hook by the porthole. Though I have already found out that it is no use to scream, he pushes a handkerchief into my mouth and ties a tie around my face so I can't spit the gag out. I try to kick, but he holds my legs down long enough to tie them together. Finally, he blindfolds me.

I hear him being busy with some tools; then he pins my legs and body hard against the wall, and I feel pricks of sharp pain on my lower abdomen.

I almost faint, but then I feel the gentlest licking on my lower belly, where the pain had been sharpest. The licking continues around my pubis and my thighs. I hear him mumble comforting words and finally feel him untie my legs. The licking continues around my clitoris and my labia—back and forth, softly licking and sucking. He lifts one of my legs and tries to push his tongue into my vagina, and then back to my lips, the clitoris, the anus, again and again, until I feel almost numb with pleasure. He keeps mumbling soothingly, and I hear him unzip and feel him push his penis into me. He puts a hand on each of my buttocks and lifts me and moves in and out of me forcefully but still very gently.

When my body reacts in such a way that he could not possibly doubt that I enjoy it, he unties my hands, takes my gag away, and, while still inside me, he carries me over to the cot. He lays me down, and we make love in every possible way, like I never have before. When we are done, he asks me my name and gives me his. Then he unties my blindfold, and I look down at the place on my lower abdomen where I had felt that terrible pain and where the licking began, and I see, just above the hair of my pubis, a blue tattoo of a three-masted ship in full sail.

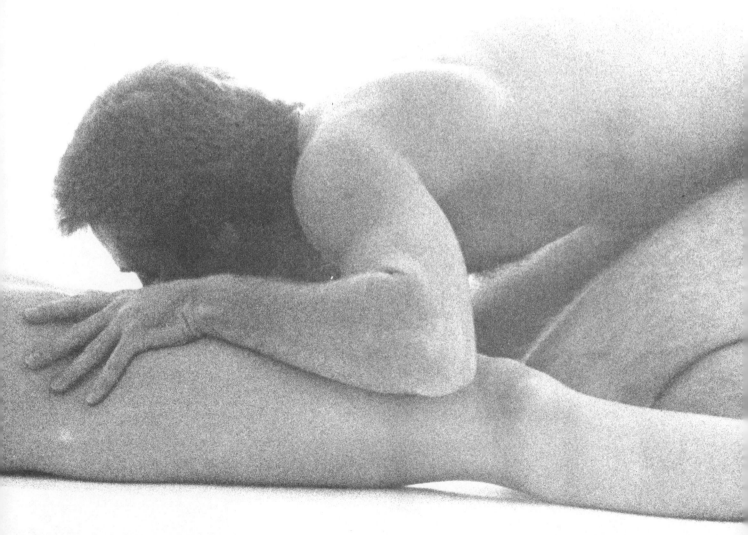

You Are What You Wear

When primitive man puts on a bearskin, a stuffed bear head, and a necklace of bear claws, he doesn't do it in order to be warm or comfortable, he does it in order to magically attain the strength of the bear. Shamans and priests among tribes in America, Tahiti, India, and the Congo wore dresses and other feminine articles. The ermine robe and the golden crown, the prayer shawl and the four-leaf clover, the bride's *something old, something new, something borrowed, something blue* are all part of an old belief in the power of the garment.

Whether you wear a tiger tooth around your neck, a ring or bracelet made of elephant hair, a wedding band, or a friendship ring, you are partaking to some degree in those old mysteries. Though clothes do not necessarily make the man, as the saying goes, clothes can determine how we feel about ourselves and others.

If you see a man wearing a cowboy shirt and hat, cowboy boots, and a belt with a silver buckle, do you think of him as a cowboy? How do you feel if you or your girl wears a black negligee? Do you feel naughty and sexy if

you walk around without underpants? Do you feel tougher and cooler in a certain hat? Do you feel more relaxed if you wear jeans as compared to a suit or fancy dress? If you go to a masquerade, do you act the part of whatever you are supposed to be according to your outfit? Would you dare to wear one of those bras that expose the nipples? If you are a male, how would you feel about wearing women's clothes?

There are some who still prefer the mysteriousness of clothes that really cover. Remember the long Victorian skirts, the high-necked blouses? Others feel sexier wearing or watching a low-cut dress and a pair of tight pants. American men still shy away from bikini bathing suits that are unlined and therefore expose the shape of their genitals, while Frenchmen ridicule the loose-fitting American pants and bathing suits. Clothes are meant to cover, to warm, to conceal, or to exaggerate certain parts of the anatomy. The codpiece of old was worn less in order to protect the male than in order to emphasize his genitals. Padded bras are worn to make the breasts look bigger.

Fashions change, and it is interesting to notice the changes, and it is fun to be aware of what you really like and what your partner likes. Whole dimensions of illusions can be connected to styles of dress or just one particular garment. Here are some stories that have been told to me.

 # The Lady of the Garter

My husband likes me to dress up in black garters and high-heeled shoes. If I do, he gets really excited and is the greatest lover. If I don't, he is just so-so. When we were first married, I thought it was strange that he wanted me to dress up, but now I like it, because when I do, he sure makes me feel good. In the afternoons, I enjoy thinking about him coming home, what I will wear after supper, and what we will do.

The Architect and the Accountant

When my partner and I first started our own firm, we had a tiny office above a dress shop. A rather plain but wholesome-looking girl who did accounting for the dress shop also did our accounting. And more than once, when my partner wasn't there, we would have a quickie on the floor or on the desk. One day when I asked her up for lunch, she showed up in a bridal outfit—long veil, a wide, lacy skirt—and under all that virginal white, she was bare-assed. Wow.

I'll never get that bride thing out of my mind. I think about it, and sometimes I imagine her coming up to see me in any of a variety of possible outfits borrowed from the dress shop. And there is always some element of surprise, like no panties under the wedding dress. Nude under a fur coat. Boots, stockings, and garter belt under a cape.

Help me
with
the buttons.

My body
is
the only clothing
I can possibly
wear.

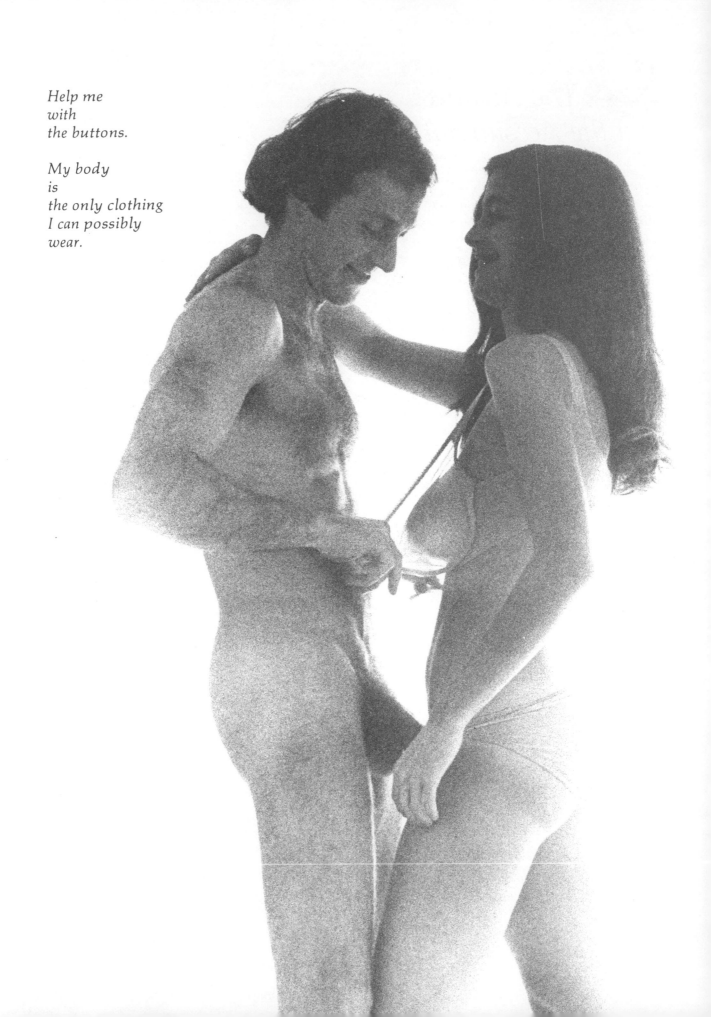

A Rose
Is a Rose Is a . . .

"My luve [love] is like a red red rose," wrote the poet Robert Burns. And for ages the lover has given his love a red red rose. Why not a white carnation?

Have you ever poked your fingers into a red rose that was opening to your touch? Did you find the center as you unfolded it, petal by petal? If you ever have unfolded a woman's flower, lip by lip, you might have sensed the similarity.

The nine-year-old daughter of a friend came upon a picture of the female genitalia and said: "Mommy, it's beautiful. It's just like a flower."

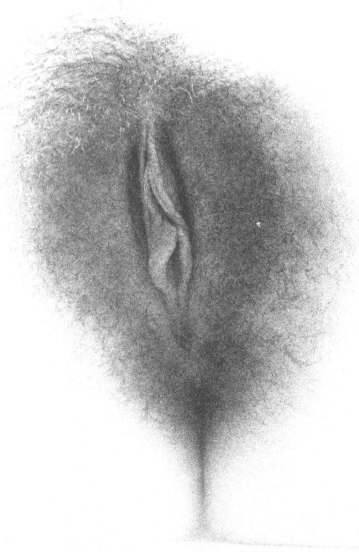

And Shakespeare wrote:
"Where the bee sucks, so shall I."

When the rose is in bud, it seems male, somehow. Maybe a flower is the perfect androgyny, changing from male to female as it opens.

Erotic awareness of flower and fruit can enhance one's thinking about sexual parts and actions, and vice versa. If you saw the movie *Tom Jones,* you probably recognized the eroticism in the scene where the lovers eat ripe, juicy pears while they lick their lips and look at each other. In China the peach is a female symbol. The Chinese peach has a deep cleft, and I am sure it is as juicy as the ripe peaches we know, and as delicious to eat.

The word *orchid* comes from the Greek word for *testicle.* A tomato used to be called a *love apple.* Pomegranates and pumpkins are symbols of fertility. Do you know the smell of persimmons?

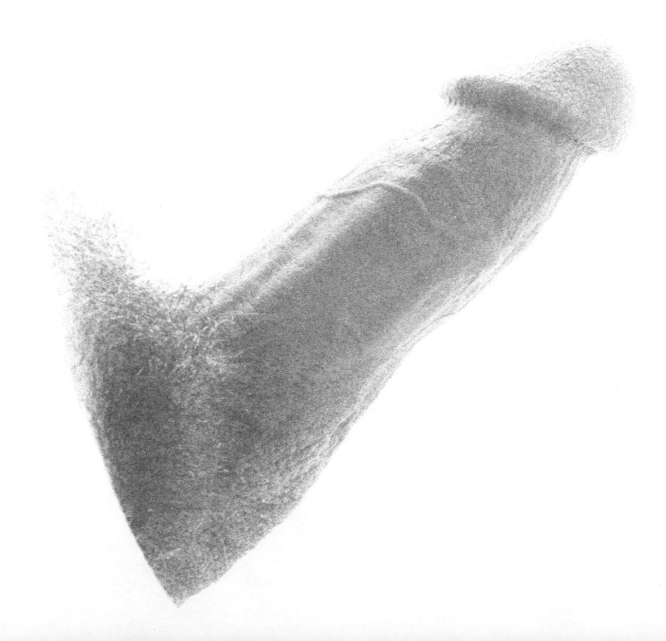

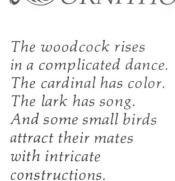ORNITHOLOGY

The woodcock rises
in a complicated dance.
The cardinal has color.
The lark has song.
And some small birds
attract their mates
with intricate
constructions.

I brush my hair,
wear bright colors and
French perfume,
and walk around
my garden,

kick a pebble and
pick a rose,
lift the rose up
to my lips
to feel a petal:
penis skin.

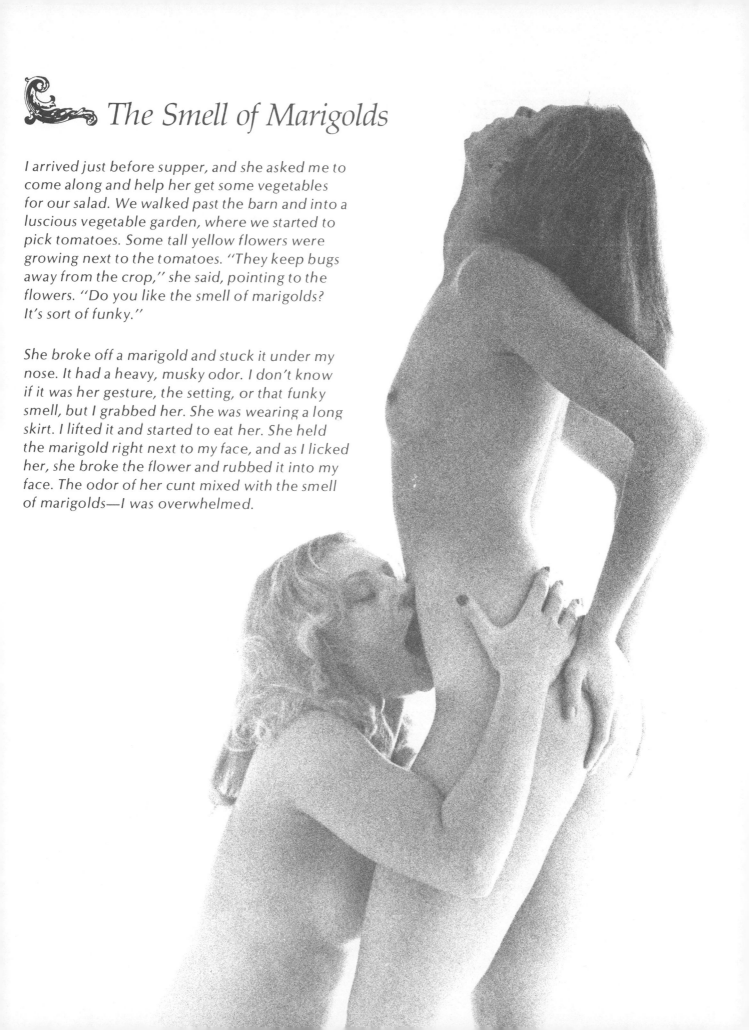

The Smell of Marigolds

I arrived just before supper, and she asked me to come along and help her get some vegetables for our salad. We walked past the barn and into a luscious vegetable garden, where we started to pick tomatoes. Some tall yellow flowers were growing next to the tomatoes. "They keep bugs away from the crop," she said, pointing to the flowers. "Do you like the smell of marigolds? It's sort of funky."

She broke off a marigold and stuck it under my nose. It had a heavy, musky odor. I don't know if it was her gesture, the setting, or that funky smell, but I grabbed her. She was wearing a long skirt. I lifted it and started to eat her. She held the marigold right next to my face, and as I licked her, she broke the flower and rubbed it into my face. The odor of her cunt mixed with the smell of marigolds—I was overwhelmed.

 # POMEGRANATES

you take me to the woods
where the sun is still warm
on brown leaves
you show me how to squeeze
the fruit
bite a small hole
and suck

fresh water sifted in soil
drawn by roots to rise
in the trunk
to be red and sweet
in the fruit
and yet sweeter
in my mouth
before I give you
to drink

 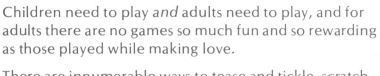

Playing

Children need to play *and* adults need to play, and for adults there are no games so much fun and so rewarding as those played while making love.

There are innumerable ways to tease and tickle, scratch and kiss, and suck and caress. Pretend she is a virgin. Pretend she is a whore. Pretend he is the bad guy with the black eye patch. Maybe he is the king of Siam, while you are the favored one in the harem. Perhaps you are just a little girl going to sleep, and he is a teddy bear, and . . . . Or you are a doctor, and he is the patient, and. . . .

You can keep your fantasies a secret, but if you verbalize them, your partner can play along.

I am going to rape you!

No. No! NO! No. YES!

I'm taking a little walk down the mountain (of your leg) and up the mountain (of your other leg) and around the side of the hill (of your hip) and over the bouncy marshland (of your breast) or through the woods (of your hairy chest), and I take a dip in a little lake (of your mouth—no, there are no monsters in this lake, don't bite!) and around the cavern (of your belly button) and into the forest (of your pubic hair), and there. . . .

Now it's MY turn to be the woman, YOU be the man. You play each other's part. If you are female, become aggressive, put the weight of your body on top of his, probe fingers into his anus and his mouth and his ears. If you are a man, sprawl on the bed, let her be the aggressive one, let yourself be entered, accept her fingers and her tongue.

This is my snake.

I'm going to eat your peach.

I am a minotaur.

I am a chimera.

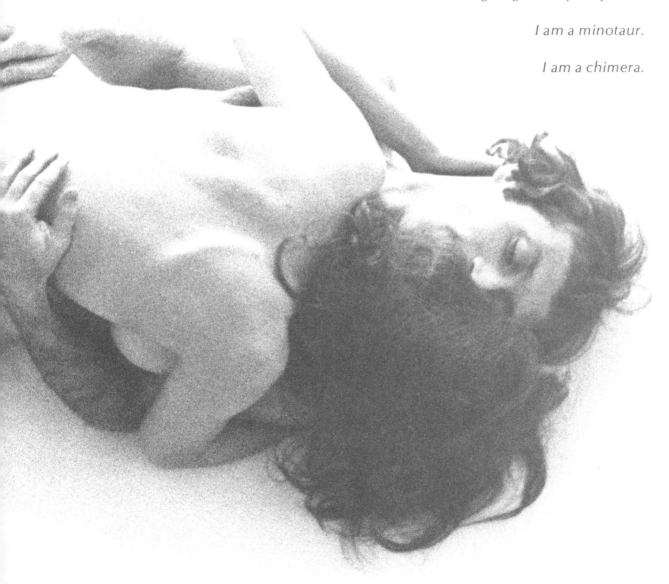

The Snake Charmer

You think the bump is sexy? Well, I'd take Mozart's flute concerto anytime. When I masturbate, I play it on the record player or I imagine I hear the music. As the flute plays, I picture myself as one of those Indian snake charmers, and my snake rises. Then, after I am hard, it doesn't matter if and what I fantasize. But the flute music seems to be an important ingredient for getting my snake going. Even when I want to make love. I sometimes think of Mozart and the snake.

MAKING LOVE TO ALICE

I imagine Gertrude making love to Alice
her generous and wise mouth upon her
breast her arms around hers the two
bodies fitting together, strangely
they are different and wonderfully they are
together. Gertrude being warm and full and
with Alice and Alice being warm and full with
Gertrude who is with her and the way
she is with her. Laughing. I imagine
they must know each other, the two, the one.

It is as with you and I. It is
with us as them. She then she and you then I
imagine. And in the act of imagining
make love to love to love to love

MARCIE HERSHMAN

 *In the Forest of the Night*

Grrrrrrr. I am a tiger. You are lying on your back, and I am crouching on the bed. We are both naked. I growl again and show my teeth. I lift my pawlike hands and scratch you on the inside of your thighs. I am sure to use my nails. I stand on all fours over you and bend my head down so that my hair covers my face as I move my head from side to side. The hair is long and tickles your skin. I tell you it is the soft fur of the tiger that touches you. I keep my hair over my face, for I believe the game will be more believable if you don't see my face.

I nuzzle your neck, your thighs, your belly. I lick your feet and your ears and your cock. I tell you I am going to eat you up, and while my nails scratch softly, I take your balls into my mouth. I growl. I move up your body and lick your eyelids and try to shape my mouth around your closed eyes. I ask you if I should eat you up and you say No. But I'm gonna eat you up, I say, and snort around your ears, take them into my mouth, growl, bite into the earlobes, and tug at them. I let my hair swish over your belly and around your genitals and ask again: "Shall I eat you up?" Now

you say Yes. I lick your penis, take all of it into my mouth, moving up and down. I let you feel my teeth scratch, then I lick it gently again. I am a good tiger.

You might have played this game before. Sometimes you try to push her away. You shiver with pleasure. You moan. You tell her you are not scared. You try to stop her. You egg her on.

Sometimes you fight back. You can be a tiger, too. You claw her back. You bury your head in her belly. You say that if she is a tiger, you are going to eat the forest of the night. You do. Then you make her stand on all fours while you enter her from behind. When you are done, you turn her over and lick her juicy slit.

 *Blindman's Buff*

I imagine it happening in some dark corner of a train or a subway station, outside a powder room, or in the basement. I am usually scared of that kind of place, but in my fantasy I am not.

He is always dark—maybe because I associate him with dark places—and I never see his face. It is either too dark for me to see it, or he has it covered with a mask. He usually approaches me from the back and just pulls me toward him. The way I think about it is the way one remembers dreams— you know, there is no connection between one scene and the next, because in the fantasy we are at first both dressed, then, the next second, we are naked and making love passionately.

This last part changes from time to time, but I never picture us lying down to make love—we are always standing up, or I am riding on his hips, or I lean over and he enters me from behind, or I am leaning against a wall or something. And then, as soon as we are done, we are dressed and he disappears again.

Dining Out—Dining In

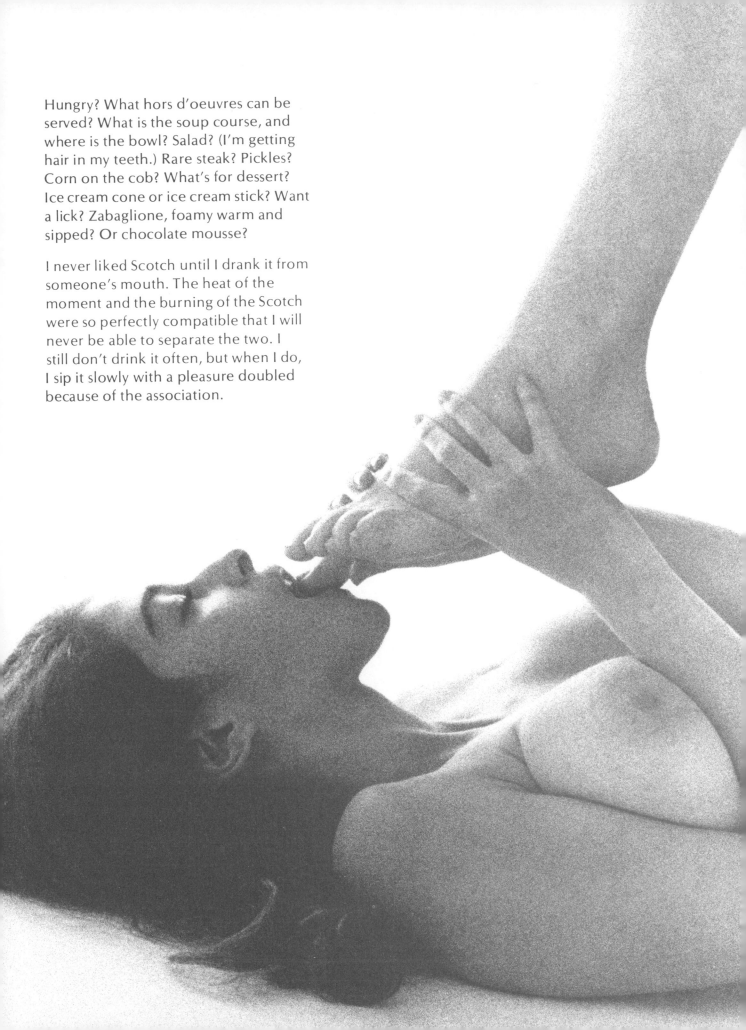

Hungry? What hors d'oeuvres can be served? What is the soup course, and where is the bowl? Salad? (I'm getting hair in my teeth.) Rare steak? Pickles? Corn on the cob? What's for dessert? Ice cream cone or ice cream stick? Want a lick? Zabaglione, foamy warm and sipped? Or chocolate mousse?

I never liked Scotch until I drank it from someone's mouth. The heat of the moment and the burning of the Scotch were so perfectly compatible that I will never be able to separate the two. I still don't drink it often, but when I do, I sip it slowly with a pleasure doubled because of the association.

One often attaches one sensual awareness with another. Seeing a picture of a woman's legs spread open, a man can conjure up the tastes and smells. Getting a whiff on a bus of a certain perfume can trigger a mental walk in search of the moment when it was first encountered. If you fall in love with someone over a Japanese dinner, you might connect the taste of raw fish and warm sake with the sound of your lover's voice, the words said, or the touch of his hand across the table.

There is a certain odor to each person's skin and hair. And the wise woman knows that her personal odors are some of her finer assets. A clean body that gets aroused will show off the stimulating odors that emanate. Though some don't like the odor of semen, most people find it erotic. Human sweat

can also be a stimulant. A nonsmoker might love the smell of smoke because his or her lover smells of smoke. If you peel and eat an orange every time you have finished making love, your lover will surely start to find the smell of oranges exciting. Next time you shower with someone and wash each other's hair, use a new shampoo. Use a powder your partner likes. Find a new fragrant oil for the next massage.

Tastes are as varied and personal. Did you ever lick the salt of someone's skin after a swim in the ocean? Have you chewed eucalyptus leaves? Grass? Nasturtiums? Or tasted the water in a mountain stream? Different parts of the body can have different tastes—the semen, the vaginal juices, the ear, the belly. The body is an interesting place to play restaurant.

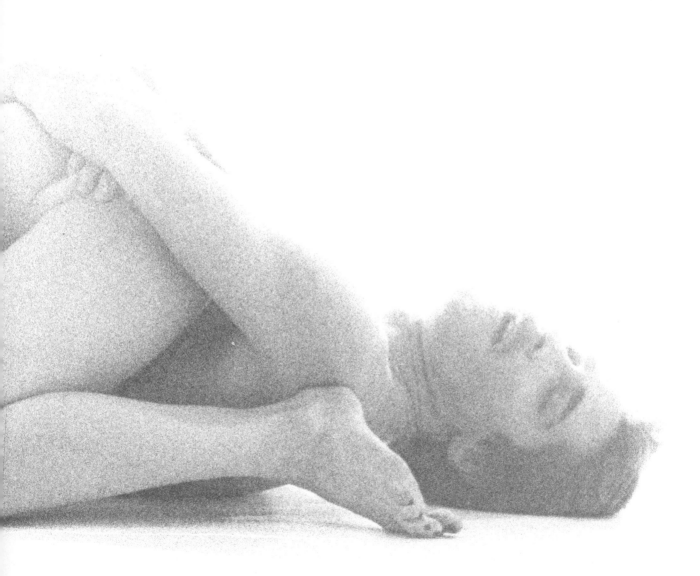

 EROTIC POEM #484

I wanted to write
this really erotic poem
about you and me
so I began with kissing

but I liked your tongue
in my mouth so much
that I never got round to the part
where I slide my hand inside your jeans
against how hot your skin is
and you go down on me
and I grab hold of your hair
and hang on just like
Australia;

because you're still just brushing
my mouth with your lips
now and then softly opening my mouth
with your tongue

and I think I am dying from this
can you die from this?
do you know?

ABIGAIL LUTTINGER

Menu for Dining Out—Dining In

Have you ever, in a crowded bar, taken a piece of ice in your mouth and kissed your lover, leaving the ice in *his* mouth?

Have you ever used a belly button as a champagne glass?

Have you ever licked warm fudge and whipped cream off someone's body?

If he asks what's for dessert, you can say: "Nipples," as you serve him raspberries, or say: "Raspberries," as you offer him your nipples.

Have you ever pushed a banana into a woman and eaten it as her motions pushed it out?

How does one talk about peaches and cream without being erotic?

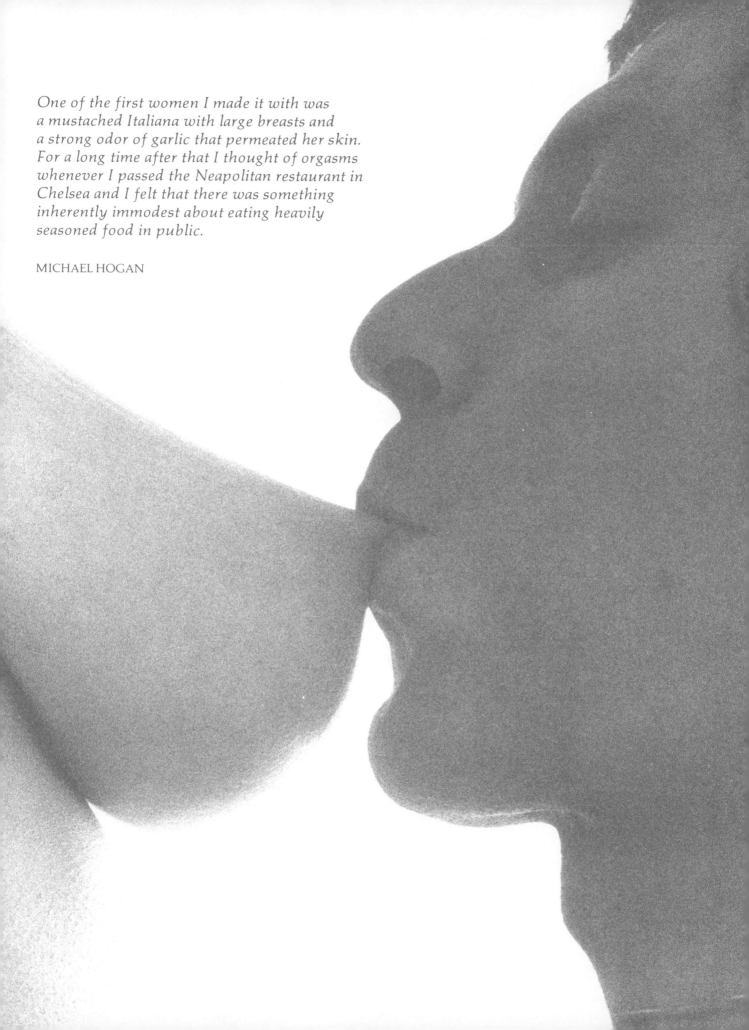

*One of the first women I made it with was
a mustached Italiana with large breasts and
a strong odor of garlic that permeated her skin.
For a long time after that I thought of orgasms
whenever I passed the Neapolitan restaurant in
Chelsea and I felt that there was something
inherently immodest about eating heavily
seasoned food in public.*

MICHAEL HOGAN

Claiming a Place

There is something almost primitive about the idea of claiming a place by making love in it. My husband and I use it as a game. New place equals new turn-on. And the fun part is that one does not actually have to be in a new place in order to enjoy the excitement of its newness. One can claim a place verbally. Pointing at a deserted beach in some Sunday paper advertisement, and saying something like "I could imagine loving you in a place like that," might lead to more than a delightful thought. One can leave the shower running and picture oneself, blatantly naked, making love by a waterfall somewhere. Your own imagination is the vehicle that can take you to the moon or the meadow, the almost too public park or the secluded mountain cabin.

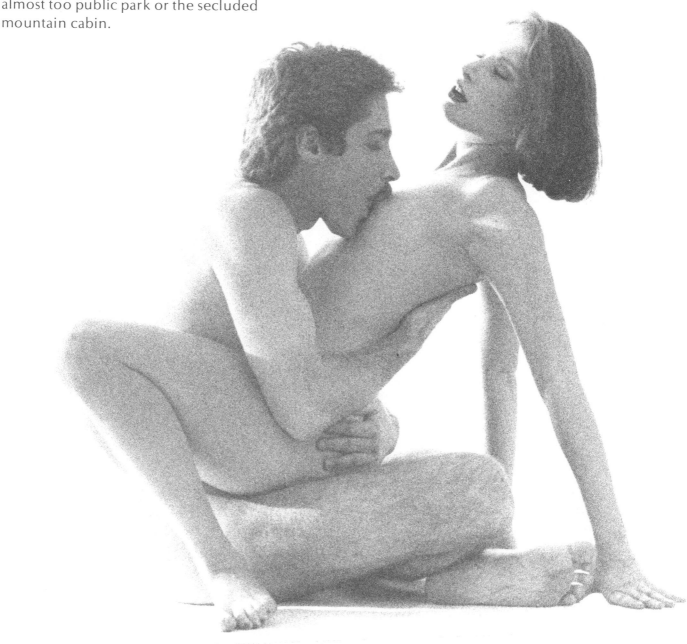

 # The Place

As I was driving up the parkway a few weeks ago, past fields of lithrum, I thought: I want to make love right there.

Lithrum is a tall flower that grows in damp places. It is often seen growing in ditches. The fact that its habitat is damp makes it even more erotic to me. Its flowers are tall spikes composed of a multitude of tiny magenta flowers. To make love in a place like that would be like being loved by the surroundings. As my lover would enter me, I would be entered by the lithrum; each magenta spear would spear me.

Somewhere there is a beach where you can go
with your love and be alone. A cove between
rocks. A tiny island offshore.

Make love where water and sand meet.
The cold water will shock you and tease you.

Make love in between the dunes, where
the air is still and hot. Become wet with each
other's sweat before you run down and
cool off in the waves.

Take handfuls of sand and rub it softly on
his belly, on her thighs.

Fly a kite. Run away from each other, catch up with each other, tackle each other.

Take a nap on the sand. Massage each other slowly, slowly with oil. Rub the toes and the fingers, the buttocks, the genitals, the neck, the nipples. Lie still in the sun for a while, feeling the sun heat the oil on your skin. I recommend coconut oil, though I warn you that its odors might make you hungry and give you an intense craving for piña coladas. Yum. Some say the best drink for the beach is a wine cooler; equal parts of cold white wine and tonic. Try it.

 Blueberry Woods

My dreams of making love in beautiful
places go way back to my childhood. I
remember lying on my back on a bed of
wild blueberries in the woods and
thinking I wanted someone to come and
make love to me right then and there.
I imagined the lovemaking and pictured
the blue stains the blueberries would
leave on my back. I forget if it was
someone special I imagined or just
anyone. Perhaps a lumberman working
in the woods? Or a boy from the village
who was as young and inexperienced as I?
The person was exchangeable, but the
place was constant, and the image of that
place keeps coming back to my mind.
I have thought about it so often that it
is as if I really have made love in that
blueberry forest.

 # A Meadow Lark

Allen tells me:

*If I see a beautiful meadow, I want
to lie in it. I can imagine the smell
of weeds and flowers, the grind of
crickets, and the buzz of the bees.
I want to see Antonio's body and hair
move as the grasses move. I want our
odors to mingle with the odors
around us. I want to hear our voices
as part of the surrounding sounds.*

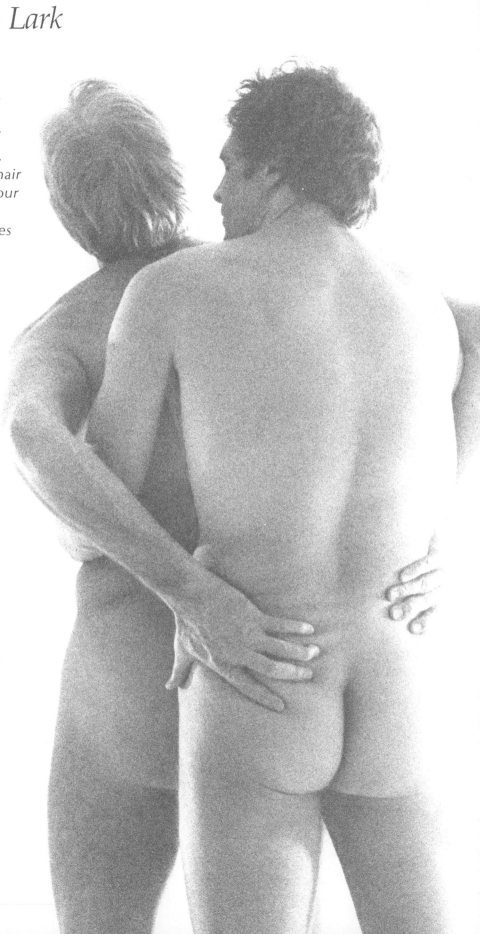

Jeannie's Story

One's own erotic memories can become one's erotic fantasies. Here is Jeannie's story.

We are on vacation, and we have a fight. I walk out of the hotel room and stand on the balcony overlooking the beach. I stand alone for a while, then my husband joins me. We say something like "It's so silly to fight, especially in a place like this." He stands behind me, and soon I can feel his erection through my nightgown. He pulls off my gown, and I am standing there naked. The lights of Honolulu and the hotels around the beach are all aglow. The surf can be heard.

I lean forward on the balustrade, and he enters me from behind. It is dark on the balcony. Could

anyone see us? Someone in some other hotel?
Someone in our hotel? Someone on the beach?
Could anyone hear the small moans that slip
out of my mouth? The unanswered questions
are part of the excitement. The unresolved
argument is part of the seduction. Our
aggressions spill away, and as we reach a climax,
we melt into the soft beauty of the night.

I am telling this in the present tense because I
relive the moments from time to time. We are
at home in our bed, and he lies behind me. I
can feel his body start to react, and I want him to
enter me. I want him to hold my breasts and love
me high above Waikiki. I want to feel him and
see the lights below me and hear the soft surge
of the surf. An image from the past melts
beautifully into the present. One could say that
the past and the present make love, as we do.

 # Desk Work

Annie and I have worked together for almost three years, and I am quite used to her charm, but one Thursday after a sales conference during which she had been both uppity and smart, we had a slight argument, and I found her irresistible. She has a way of tilting her head sideways and up when she is angry, a motion that is both childlike and challenging. So I grabbed her. That's all that happened, but I sure like to imagine it going further.

I picture Annie on her back on the desk answering phone calls and trying to sound cool while I do every conceivable kind of thing to excite her. I picture papers and files falling off the desk, a secretary knocking on the door, the boss calling for a consultation while we are giggling and fucking through it all.

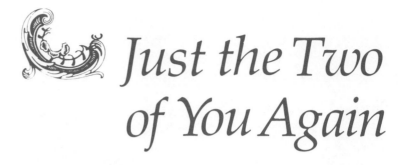

Just the Two of You Again

If you have raised a child, or two, or three, and the time comes when the last child leaves for college, work, or marriage, that time can be used as a time of rediscovery.

As a parent, you might have wanted a quiet and proper home life for your family. You and your spouse might have limited your sexual overtures and acts to the bedroom. Now that there are just the two of you again, you will probably enjoy becoming more open with each other verbally and sexually. You can start by reclaiming the

house. Make love in the TV room. Make love in the sauna. Have breakfast in the nude. Attract each other verbally by saying something like "There is no reason why we shouldn't make love in the living room." Try the hammock, the rocking chair, the kitchen. Reclaim the phonograph and play the music *you* like, as compared to the music the kids preferred.

This is a time in life when most couples live with more financial ease. If this is the case, take advantage of it. If one of you must go on a business trip, invite the other along and make it into a vacation. Plan a midweek lunch at a museum or some intimate little restaurant. Buy her a ridiculously sexy black nightie. Buy him a flowered tie and tell him it reminds you of the Polynesian island where you would like to take him.

And be naughty now and then. If all those years
ago you made love in the car, try it again.

A man who has been used to throwing a football
with a son might miss that informal playing
out-of-doors. Maybe he needs a playmate. Learn
a new sport together: tennis, paddleball, skiing,
jogging, hiking, or even just an occasional walk.

Pamper her. When was the last time you
massaged her body?

Surprise him. Send him a letter at his office.
Plan a picnic for two.

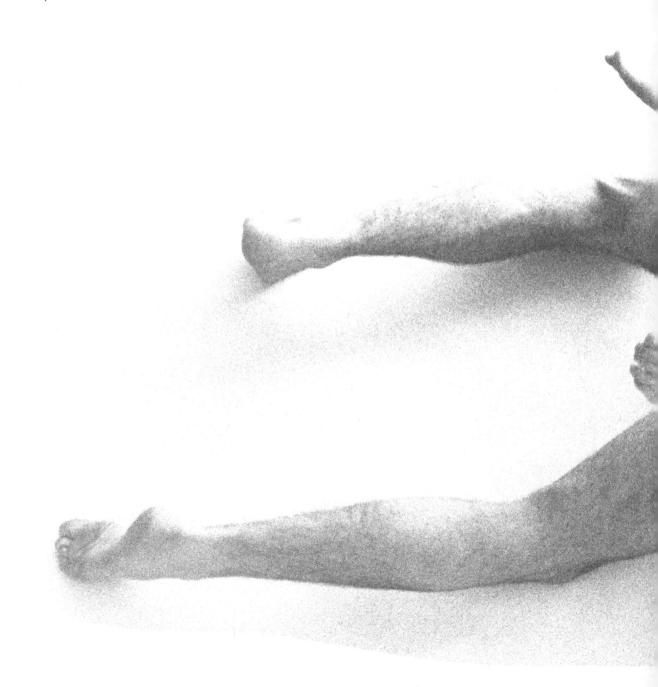

YOU & I POEM

U U U U U
U U U U
U U U
U U
I

CHARLES LEVENDOSKY

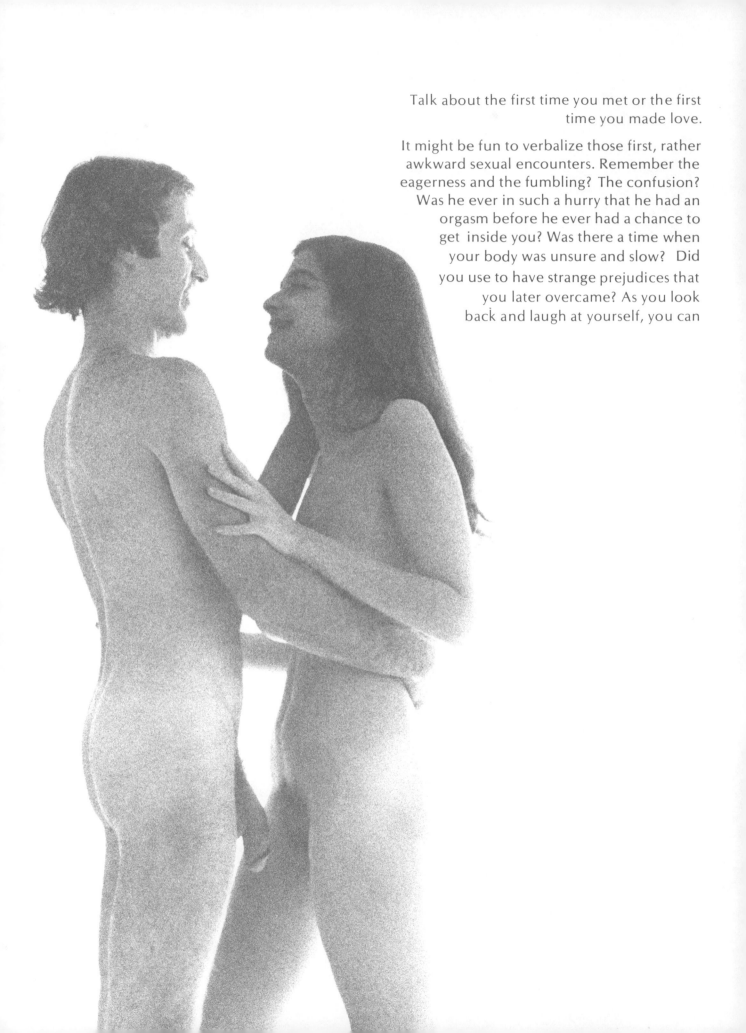

Talk about the first time you met or the first time you made love.

It might be fun to verbalize those first, rather awkward sexual encounters. Remember the eagerness and the fumbling? The confusion? Was he ever in such a hurry that he had an orgasm before he ever had a chance to get inside you? Was there a time when your body was unsure and slow? Did you use to have strange prejudices that you later overcame? As you look back and laugh at yourself, you can get to know yourself, as well as your partner, better. Happy memories shared can act as a kind of verbal affection.

Remember the time when Tommy walked in on us and asked: Why are you squashing mommy?

Remember that Sunday morning when Wendy caught us in bed and said: "I want to wrestle, too."

Become each other's dates and lovers again.

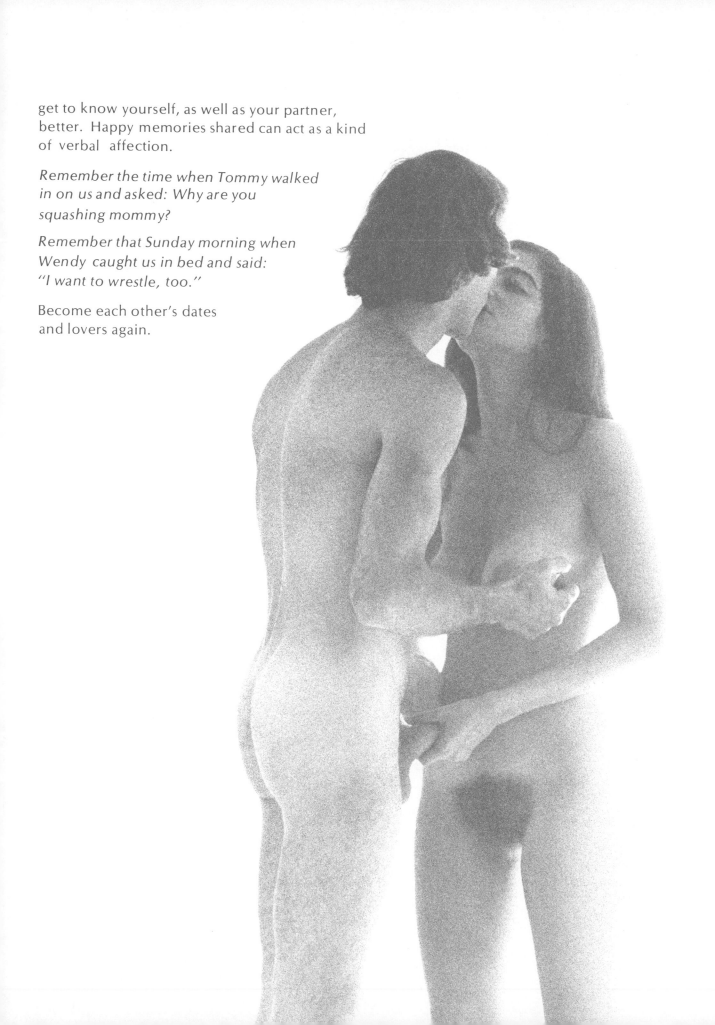

The young girls look up
as we walk past the line at the movie,
and go back to examining their fingernails.

Their boy friends are combing their hair,
and chew gum
as if they meant to insult us.

Today we made love all day.
I look at you. You are smiling at the sidewalk,
dear wrinkled face.

DONALD HALL

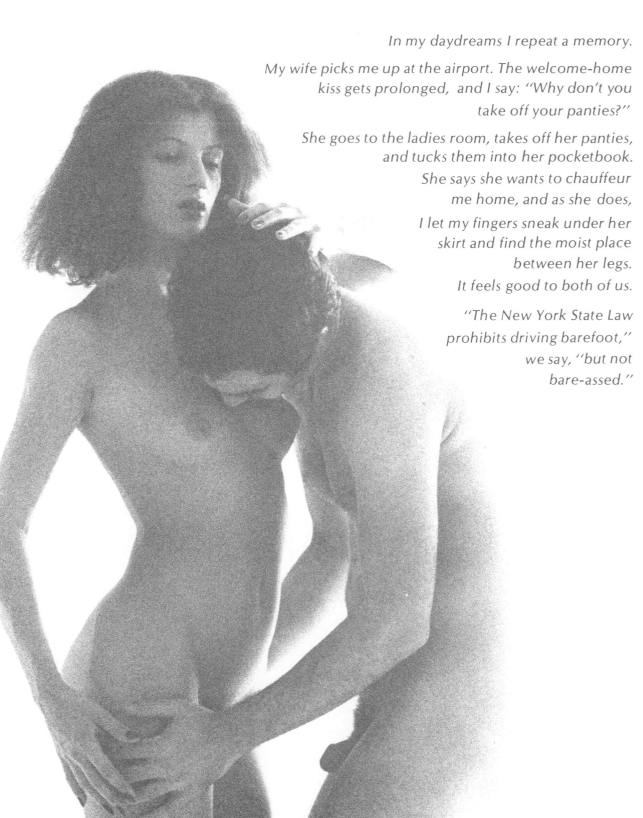

 Welcome Home

In my daydreams I repeat a memory.

My wife picks me up at the airport. The welcome-home kiss gets prolonged, and I say: "Why don't you take off your panties?"

She goes to the ladies room, takes off her panties, and tucks them into her pocketbook. She says she wants to chauffeur me home, and as she does,

I let my fingers sneak under her skirt and find the moist place between her legs. It feels good to both of us.

"The New York State Law prohibits driving barefoot," we say, "but not bare-assed."

 # Making a Baby

The time of pregnancy can be a very special time for a couple. The realization that their lovemaking is producing something beyond pleasure is bound to provoke amazement and pride. The idea that *they* are part of the whole complex chain of creation might fill them with both awe and gratitude. Imagine—really, actually *creating* a baby!

It is true that a pregnant woman might have trouble with nausea during the early part of the pregnancy. She might feel unusually sleepy at times, and she will probably feel heavy and awkward at the end of the pregnancy. Her bigness might give her backaches, and her growing belly might put pressure on the bladder, yet it is a fact that many woman experience

increased erotic interest during this time. It is also a fact that many women who used to be nonorgasmic learn to achieve orgasm, and monoorgasmic women change to polyorgasmic women during pregnancy.

The heightened eroticism that some pregnant women know is not only found in women who are happily married. It has also been observed in unmarried women and women who live alone. There is something to the old saying that links pregnancy and contentment. A friend who is forty-one and experiencing her first pregnancy is glowing with joy and beauty. Many men love the bigness of a pregnant woman. A man I know recently told me, in reference to his wife and the pregnancy: "I just want to be with her and touch her all the time!"

A woman told me: "I especially love it when I get into bed at night. I lie on my back and watch my big belly. The baby seems to notice that I am not sitting or standing anymore, and he seems to delight in the new position. I lie there and watch him turn somersaults, and I imagine a leg here and buttocks there. It is as if we are communicating. Maybe it sounds silly, but I actually think we are communicating."

The Dream Come True

Ever since I got pregnant, I seem to be spending so much time daydreaming. It is as if my whole life has something new around which to dream. I think about playing with the child. I think about the things I will teach him, the flowers I will name, the constellations I will show him how to find. No, I don't spend much time wondering if he will be president, but I do wonder if he will have Howard's ear for music or my voice, if he will be tall like my father or a redhead like my sister.

The child is a kind of "dream come true" for me, and in my daydreams I continue to fulfill my dreams. I picture myself walking in the woods with the child, and I show him how soft the moss is, how large some of the leaves are, how tiny the wild flowers, how sharp the pine needles are, and how scratchy the bark is. I tell him the names of every tree, bush, berry, and bird. I tell him about the pixies that drink from the goblet lichen.

I must have imagined every important event in his life: birthday parties and holidays, first trip to the beach and first trip in a plane. Yes, everything I think about turns into a daydream about the child.

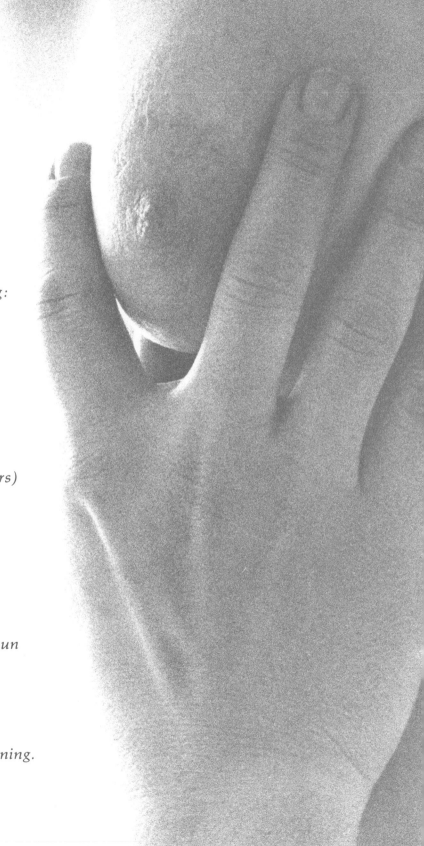

 MATINS

I

In the small of the morning
I want to wake, to bring you something:
the call of the morning dove,

soft like that
or the light where your shoulder
meets the pillow.

II

If I cannot find flowers, two handfuls
of berries (the bushes scratch my fingers)
or a cup of spring

water, should I return, emptyhanded,
my breasts to fill the cups
of your fingers?

III

I used to sleep late, to wake when the sun
was high as a daughter should be
tall and fair;

now I wake early and know,
writing this poem tells me,
I should bring you the child in the morning.

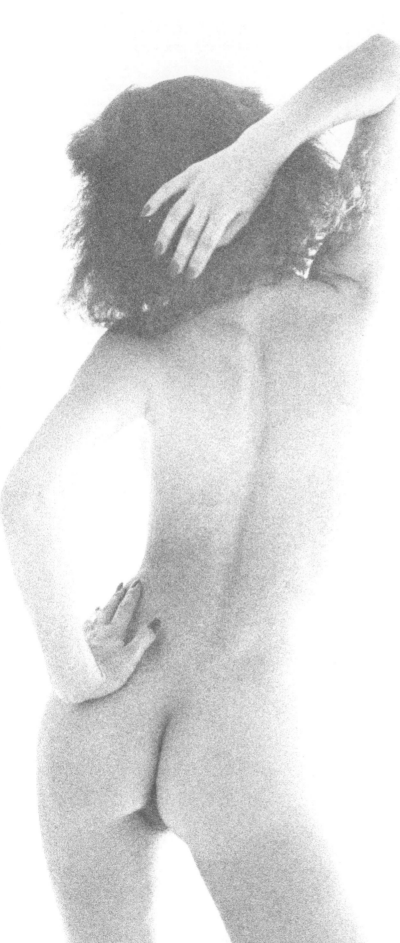

Walk in Beauty

After I have done my morning work, I take off my clothes, and shower. If it is summer, I wrap a towel around me and walk out to the pool. I let the towel drop on the grass, and enter the pool naked. My husband and I designed this pool, and it is very beautiful. It is a granite-edged black pool, and there is always a touch of magic in the moment of entering its reflection. Because the pool is dark, the surface becomes a mirror that holds the flowering trees, or the clouds, or the stone walls of the house.

I let my hands reach out in front of me to pull me through the water, and I like to watch my hands disturb the surface, exchanging the one image of its reflection for a hundred moving images. As I swim back and forth, I observe the sky and the clouds. Sometimes a dragonfly is my visitor. Sometimes a bird can be seen building a nest. Sometimes I purposely wear my lavender towel down to the pool and leave it on the edge. I like to watch the reflection of the lavender broken by the waves.

I am conscious of the beauty I see, and the visual pleasure adds to the sensual pleasure of the touch of the water. It caresses my arms and my legs and my back. I feel my breasts undulate in the motions of the waves. The water's many fingers touch my neck and the inside of my thighs. It touches my cheeks and my vulva. I become so completely immersed in the sensuality that it seems that if I opened my mouth and let the water in, it would flow right through me and come out through my vagina. If the water is warm, it is the most gentle and soothing lover. It makes me feel lazy and relaxed. If it is cold, it seems to slap my skin and rough me up, leaving me invigorated and alert.

There is an American Indian poem that goes like this:

> *Above me beauty*
> *Below me beauty*
> *I walk in beauty*
> *I am beauty*

These words sometimes come to mind as I move through my day. I often purposely create a setting that is beautiful, and as I enter that beauty, it makes me feel beautiful. It is something I can share with others, but I also can enjoy it by myself. I eat lunch alone with a book and a vase of flowers. I make a breakfast tray complete with a rose before I go back to bed to read or write. Home alone in the evening, I take a perfumed bath, sit on the sheepskin rug in front of the fire in the bedroom fireplace, and play my dulcimer. The warmth of the fire, the smell of my skin, the soft fur under my bare buttocks, the notes I pluck out of the dulcimer are all pleasures I give myself. Alone, I am in the sensual company of myself.

 *Going West*

My friend Sarah writes me:

Ever since I went across country on the motorbike, I like to relive the time. I imagine sitting behind Paul, my arms around him, the wind pulling at my hair. I am conscious of the softness of my body under the cool leather, and the vibration of the bike makes me aware of my nipples and my cunt.

We drive on and on—fields of grain, hills, cities in sunsets. I imagine us making love out there, far away, somewhere where we will be surprised by the quality of the landscape—bare rocks or lush underbrush. Smells of trucks and factories, manure, fresh-baked bread, and flowers flow over us. The skies change above, and the road rolls away under us. Yes, I travel that road again and again and again.

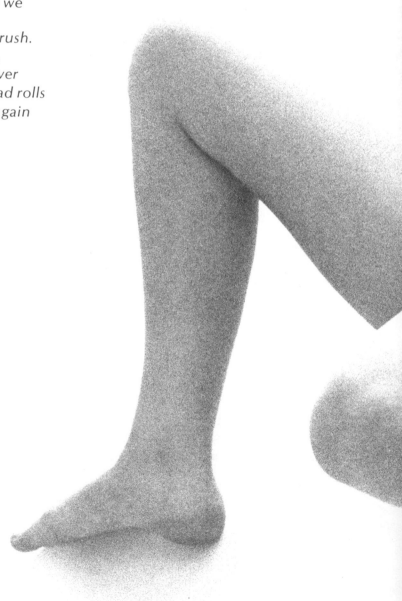

# The Thing as Itself

In a chapter about masturbation in a book about women's sexual fantasies, it says that masturbation without fantasy is unhappy and unreal. It says that without fantasy, masturbation would be "too lonely." I do not think that is true at all. Some people like to fantasize, while others like to concentrate on the very facts of the situation.

In a discussion of the subject, a friend told me that if she touches herself with her fingers, she thinks about the pleasure her own fingers can give her. If she lets the water from the hand shower play over her genitals, she thinks about making love to the water. If she uses a carrot, she looks at and thinks about the carrot. She claims to have a special love for fruits and vegetables. Sometimes she peels a cucumber and cuts off part of its tip before inserting it into her vagina. She says she likes the idea of the cucumber seeds coming off inside her. To her, the thrill is the very idea of making love to a cucumber.

Another friend, who describes a similar enjoyment of fruits and vegetables, told me that after she has used a vegetable she sometimes eats it. On occasion, she has washed the carrot or zucchini after using it, and put it back in the vegetable drawer, enjoying the idea that someone who does not know where it has been will eat it.

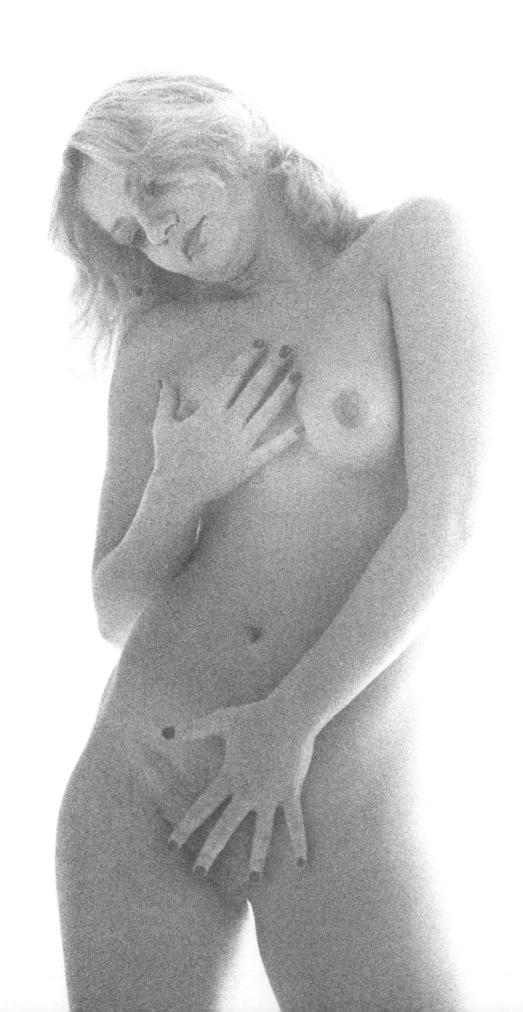

Japanese Massage

A male friend told me the following:

Once when I was in Japan on business, my host took me to one of those bath-and-massage places. I had never been to any kind of prostitute, and I didn't want to go this time; so, when the woman, after the bath, let me know we could fuck, I shook my head No. She was persistent, but I was, too. Then she said: "Massage?" and I nodded. She gave me a massage from top to toe, and then she lay down on my back, naked, and rubbed my back with her small tits. It was incredibly sexy. And then—I don't know exactly how—she slipped her toes under my balls, and somehow or other that was so erotic it finished me off. I don't masturbate often, but when I do, I think about the Japanese massage.

 # Peekaboo

Though the word *voyeur* refers to someone who looks upon (looks upon?) sex essentially as a spectator sport, there is a touch of the voyeur in all of us. We do watch as strangers kiss good-bye at the airport, we don't look away when we see the lovers in the park, and some interesting phrase can induce us to listen to the continuation of a conversation overheard at a restaurant or in a bus. The fact is that many of us first learned about sex accidentally, from some overheard conversation or some scene we chanced upon: a window or a door left open. And such accidental encounters can titillate enough to bring on both fantasy and action.

I overheard a woman say: "I keep telling Annie she shouldn't strut around the house naked like that. Anyone could see her. She says that if they want to look, let them look. If you ask me, I think she likes the idea of someone watching."

 # The Telescope

There is a new guy in the corner apartment on the fifteenth floor across the courtyard. I have bought a telescope so I can really watch him. The other day when it was so hot, he was walking around naked all day. What a bod! He did exercises in the morning, standing on his head, toes up and prick flopping toward his face, and in the afternoon he was in the kitchen. I saw him pour himself a cold beer, then watched as he licked some foam that was overflowing the glass. I could just imagine him licking me like that.

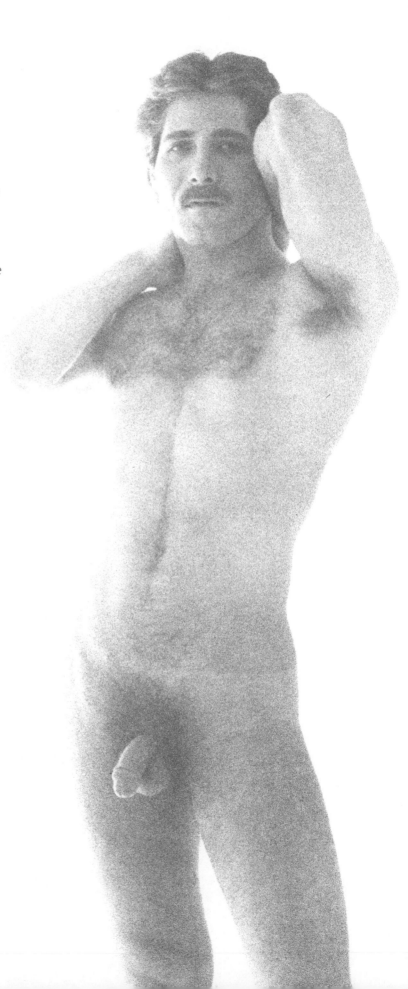

 ## The Keyhole

I don't know if I should tell you, but when I was a kid I used to peek through the keyhole on the door to my parents' bedroom to try to see what they were doing in bed. I never did see them—the door wasn't in the right place. But we had a servant couple working for us—she was cook and he was chauffeur—and a couple of times I looked through their keyhole and saw them at it. They were both fat and laughed a lot. He would be pumping away, and she would laugh and squeal with delight. I still like the idea of peeking through keyholes. When I look at girlie magazines, I imagine the girl is real and that I look at her through a keyhole and she is fucking away. And guess who she is doing it with? Me.

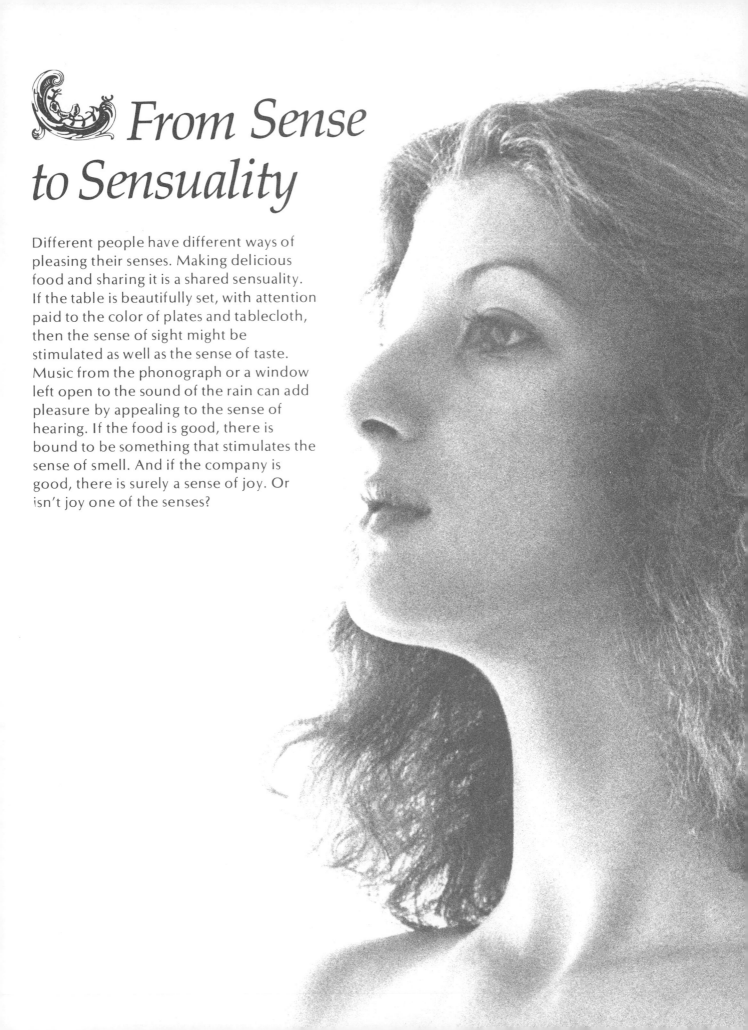

From Sense to Sensuality

Different people have different ways of pleasing their senses. Making delicious food and sharing it is a shared sensuality. If the table is beautifully set, with attention paid to the color of plates and tablecloth, then the sense of sight might be stimulated as well as the sense of taste. Music from the phonograph or a window left open to the sound of the rain can add pleasure by appealing to the sense of hearing. If the food is good, there is bound to be something that stimulates the sense of smell. And if the company is good, there is surely a sense of joy. Or isn't joy one of the senses?

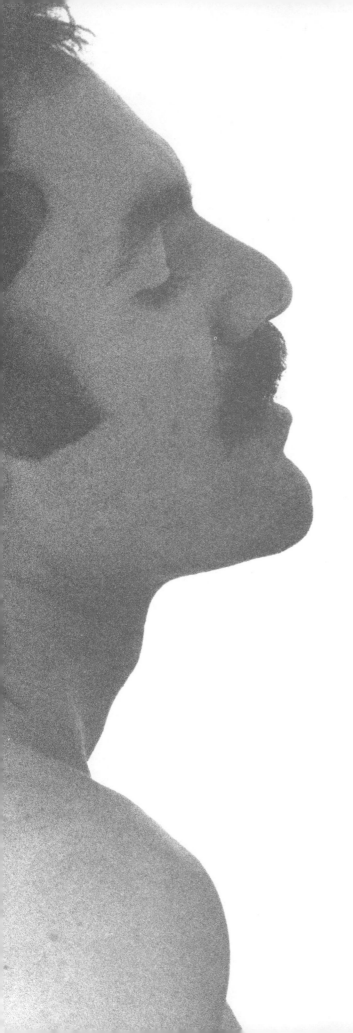

There is so much that can be enjoyed sensually, alone. Skiing, skating, hitting the perfect serve in tennis, flying a plane, driving a favorite car, riding a bike downhill—each action has its own sensuality. Think of riding a bike and feeling the wind against your face, or skiing downhill and feeling the motion of your body doing its turns. Have you known the exhilaration of hitting a ball just right, feeling how muscle and tendon work together? Or do you like hearing the hum of the engine, the vibration of the vehicle, the smells of wind, gasoline, cockpit? What do you like to do alone that is sensually pleasing?

Do you ever give yourself a treat? A pot full of crocuses when there is still snow on the ground? A glass of wine? A soft, silky blouse? A warm bath at the end of the day? A good cigar? A walk in the woods because it is autumn and the trees are turning? When did you last make an angel in the snow?

All around us there are things to touch (as I list these, think about the feel of each): towels, pillows, a slip, a peach, a sun-warm rock, sand, a dog, an icicle, a baby. And things to smell: mowed grass, burning leaves, a river, a candle, the spring thaw, a newspaper, beer, an apple, a kitchen, a tulip, a seashell. And sounds: an owl, a sea gull, traffic, "Taxi!," a train whistle, a train, a leaking faucet, the rain in the gutter, a river, a brook, the sea, leaves in the fall, palm trees in the wind, grasses, crickets, mosquitoes, dogs barking, people calling, kids, jump-rope rhymes, a bat hitting a ball, a ball hitting a glove, a baseball game, "BEER HERE," a plane overhead. And things to see? Well, you make the list and think about them, for I am sure one can educate one's senses to be more sensual, to hear, see, feel, smell more, and have a sharper sense of taste. The education starts with an awareness of what one does sense. Then it is easy to go on to sense more and more, to live a life of sensuality.

Pinwheel

I am sitting here thinking about all the genitals stirred into the spaghetti sauces of America. Women wash floors repeating the touch of their husbands. Teenage girls walk in the rain dreaming of wet kisses. Men drive to work unraveling mile after mile of conquests. Grandmothers bounce imaginary babies on their laps. Sanity is kept in the subway because someone's body was warm: a comfortable wife, a pregnant woman, a lean young man. These moments save us, walk us through the opening door, the closed conversation. The hand that held the breast in the dark, the finger that touched whatever secret place, the lips that spoke with words or movement repeat themselves through the day in the supermarket, in the factory, in the head of the father playing with his son, in the brain of the woman feeding the computer. We are all movie producers running the reels of memory and dream in our heads. It is the unspoken language of our age speaking.

It is this language that I would like to bring to the page honestly. I had been looking forward to the new year. All traveling and visiting done, all houseguests gone, I would have long days to myself and my writing. But my daughter suggested we go skiing, so we did. Actually, going skiing is consistent with my original intent, because it is the sensual images I know, that I would like to explore, and skiing is pure sensuality.

I get to the top of that first mountain wondering if I will be able to stand on the skis—and then I start downhill. The body remembers the motion, a kind of serpentine gliding through the air. Hips and shoulders control the dance. Under strange layers of clothing, my body becomes ultimately beautiful. I spread my arms out and glide down the hill singing.

The days get better and better. My daughter is seventeen, and I am thirty-five. We are teenagers and talk about the blond moustaches we see in the lift line; we ride the chair lift and giggle at the action on the slope below us. We are grown women and talk about our men, our fathers, the books we read, Jung, our dreams. We talk about our bodies and the very personal challenge of the mountain. We tease each other. We praise each other. We race each other.

I like my daughter. I braid her beautiful hair in the morning, as I did when she was small. I like Judy, my sister-in-law, who lives in the small farmhouse where we are staying. A trapper comes to pick up some chickens. A lamb is born. Judy jumps up and down with joy and hugs us all, including the trapper. The lamb is so tiny—skinny legs, huge ears, the umbilical cord still hanging from his belly. He butts his mother's udder and starts to suckle. The mother licks his anus to stimulate him. Judy says: "Maybe if I call him Lambchop I will have the heart to eat him in the spring." The father ram tries to keep everyone away.

I am telling you these things for a reason. The weekend continues—more downhill skiing, a long herbal bath, a conversation with Judy about affection, a conversation with

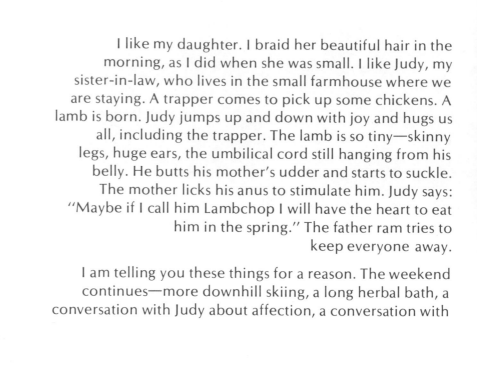

Peter about the light and space of a room. And cross-country skiing—waxing the skis, eight of us going in a file up the hill behind the house, past the sugar shack, under the striped shadows of maples, and on through a meadow, the snow glittering in the sun, past tracks of weasel and deer, fox, dog, field mouse, rabbit, up and up. Then down, down, laughing and falling. And through all these images of family, friends, animals, woods, white fields of snow, the image of you was always present. Your hands, your legs, your genitals, your face, your messed-up hair was spinning like a pinwheel slowly, slowly, in front of my face. And somewhere near the center of the pinwheel, your eyes were looking, looking at me. You were the unspoken language, the pinwheel I saw the rest of the world through, the genitals in the spaghetti, the naked bodies in the subway.

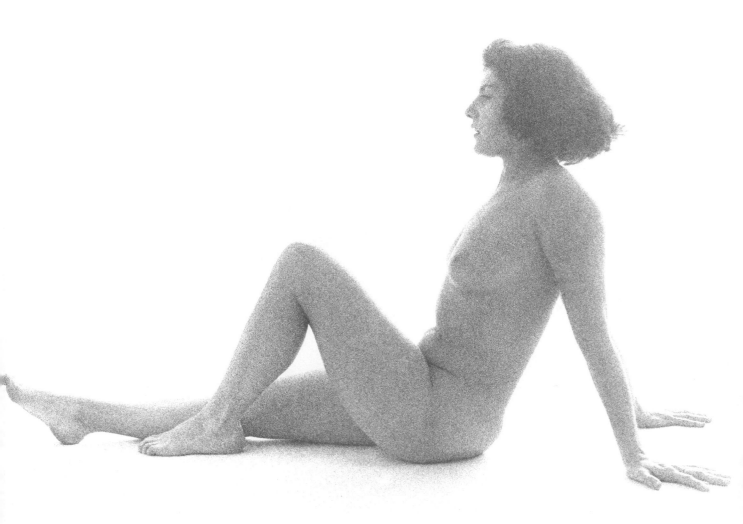

And will you understand if I say that when we are together in bed, my daughter's eyes spin on the pinwheel, her long hair is braided, snowy fields fall over our skin where we glide. I touch the rain to your lips. I am conversations of space under your hands. My body beautiful with slopes moves over you and under you. A lamb is born. A mother licks it. Strange herbs wash us clean.

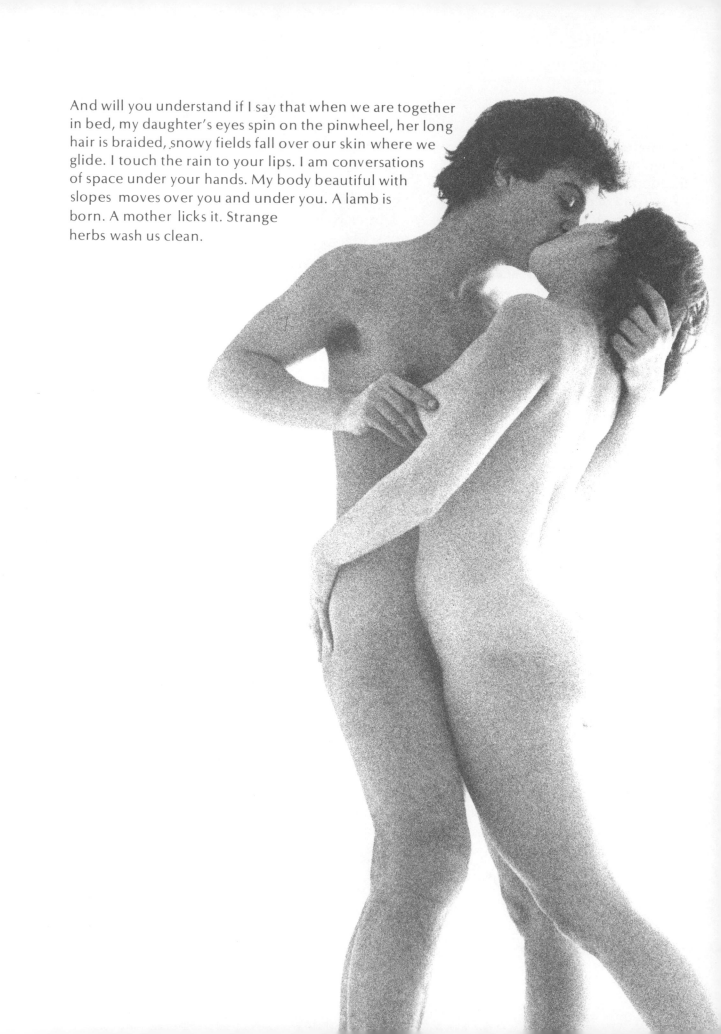

To my dear cousin, Bill Bickel, who encouraged
me to dream impossible dreams.
Your memory will always be a blessing to me.
— N.C.

To Mom, who always comes to my rescue.
— Y.N.

Text copyright © 2021 Nancy Churnin
Illustrations copyright © 2021 Yevgenia Nayberg
Cover and internal design by Simon Stahl

Library of Congress Control Number: 2021930924

Published by Creston Books, LLC
www.crestonbooks.co

ISBN 978-1-939547-95-8
Source of Production: 1010 Printing
Printed and bound in China
5 4 3 2 1

A QUEEN TO THE RESCUE

The Story of Henrietta Szold, Founder of Hadassah

By Nancy Churnin

Illustrated by
Yevgenia Nayberg

Creston Books

From the time Henrietta was little, she loved hearing about the woman who risked her life to save others. While her sisters twirled in sparkly Purim skirts, Henrietta marveled at Esther, who told a king to stop the wicked, powerful Haman from hurting her people.

As children swung groggers — noisemakers — and gobbled hamenstashen, Henrietta wondered if one day she'd have the courage to stand up and make a difference, too. After all, Esther had shown her the way.

When she was born in 1860 in Baltimore, girls weren't supposed to be brave or make a difference. The Civil War raged until she was five. The air was thick with tears for lost loved ones, with pleas from people who had escaped slavery, needing food, work, a chance to learn to read and write.

Henrietta was proud of her mother and her father, a rabbi, who helped everyone they could.

Henrietta helped, too. But as she grew older, she saw that women didn't have the same chance to make a difference that men did. Women couldn't vote, own a business, be doctors or lawyers. The only way a woman could make a difference was to get married and have children.

But Henrietta didn't marry. Or have children. Instead, in 1877, right out of high school, she became a teacher. She stayed late, working hard to help her students. Then, in the late 1800s, boatloads of Jewish immigrants flooded the streets. They'd fled violence in Poland and Russia, escaping their own Hamans, hoping for a new chance at life in America.

"Go home!" some people yelled. Others grumbled that the ragged families didn't belong in America. Henrietta could taste the fear of the newcomers.

How would they get good jobs? How would they feed their children? Henrietta thought and thought.

Then it came to her. She could make a difference by opening a school for adults. A night school — where she could teach the newcomers English after they finished work. Her school was the first of its kind, offering an important way for immigrants to learn the language and adjust to their new home.

Whenever Henrietta saw a need, she organized and worked until she made a difference. There weren't enough Jewish books? In 1893, she became the first editor for the Jewish Publication Society.

In 1912, shaken by the disease and hunger she saw in Palestine, she met with a group of women on Purim to found a charity. She gave her new organization Queen Esther's Hebrew name: *Hadassah*.

In its first year, Hadassah raised enough money to send two nurses to Jerusalem and treat 5,000 children. Henrietta moved to Palestine to oversee the work. She spent long days making sure people of every faith received heathcare, food, and education.

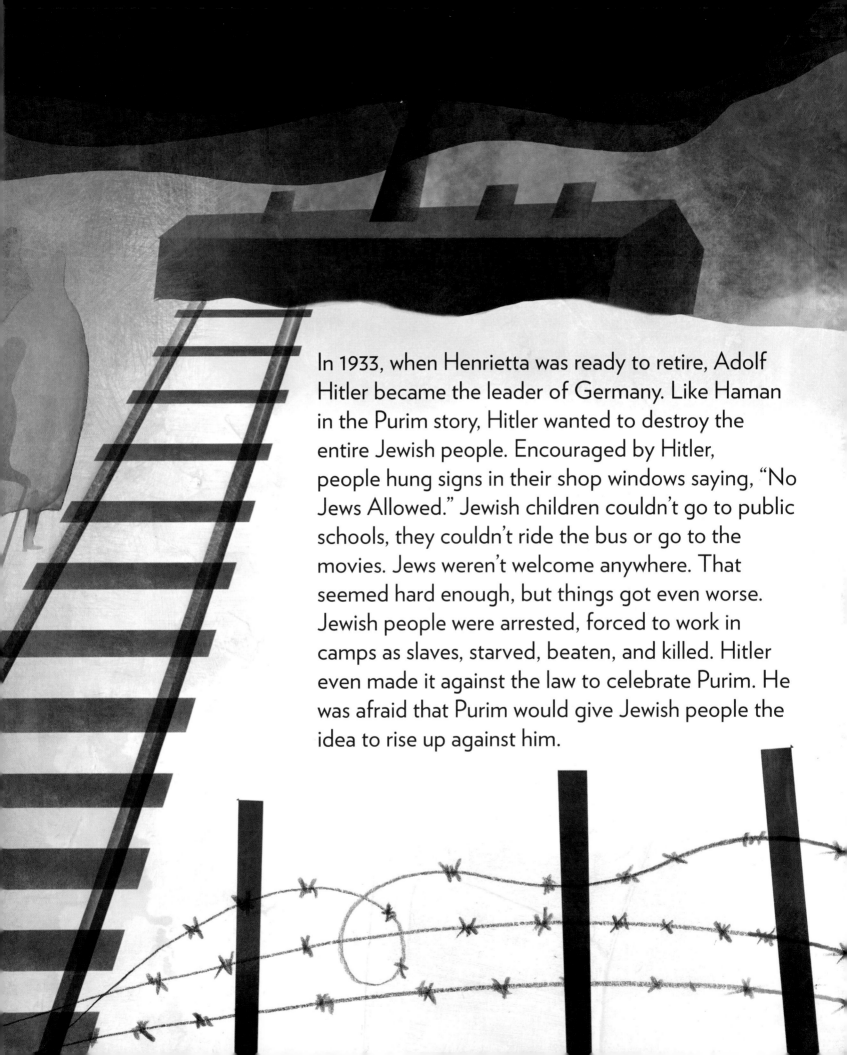

In 1933, when Henrietta was ready to retire, Adolf Hitler became the leader of Germany. Like Haman in the Purim story, Hitler wanted to destroy the entire Jewish people. Encouraged by Hitler, people hung signs in their shop windows saying, "No Jews Allowed." Jewish children couldn't go to public schools, they couldn't ride the bus or go to the movies. Jews weren't welcome anywhere. That seemed hard enough, but things got even worse. Jewish people were arrested, forced to work in camps as slaves, starved, beaten, and killed. Hitler even made it against the law to celebrate Purim. He was afraid that Purim would give Jewish people the idea to rise up against him.

Henrietta may have been old, but she was as determined as ever. She realized this was the moment she'd prepared for all her life. She could help save her people, as Queen Esther had. Henrietta took a boat to Germany right away, determined to get exit visas from German ambassadors and entrance visas from the British leaders who ran Palestine, to bring children to safety.

She knew she could be attacked or arrested at any time as she met secretly with crying parents, begging them to let their children go to a country they'd never seen to be cared for by Henrietta, whom they'd just met.

She got visas for 63 children. Meanwhile, the women who ran Hadassah raised money for their passage, care, and schooling.

Back in Palestine, Henrietta kept fighting for visas and boats to carry the children to freedom. In 1942, while World War II raged, Henrietta heard of 870 Jewish children who'd escaped from Siberian slave labor camps and were trapped in Iran. Henrietta went straight to Lord Halifax, the British ambassador to the U.S., begging him to let the children go to Palestine. Halifax didn't understand why so much fuss was being made over some ragged children, but he agreed.

On February 18, 1943, the children arrived at Port Said, Egypt, bone thin, scared, their faces blank, their spirits beaten. Henrietta greeted each by name. Seeing the sadness in their eyes, she led the children in a dance of the hora, knowing by the end every one of them would be smiling.

She found them all homes. Henrietta and her friends in Hadassah saved 11,000 children in a program called Youth Aliyah. Henrietta never had children of her own, but everywhere she went, the children she'd saved hugged her and called her "ima," Hebrew for "mom."

She loved watching them dress up to tell the story of Purim. Henrietta had been brave like Queen Esther, speaking up to save her people. And now maybe, as these children grew, they'd know what she'd always known — that Purim wasn't just about a queen from long ago, but a reminder that every one of them, boys and girls, could stand up, be brave, and make a difference, too.

"Dare to dream, and when you dream, dream big."
— Henrietta Szold

Author's Note

Henrietta Szold (Dec. 21, 1860-Feb. 13, 1945) spent a lifetime helping others and changing what was possible for women. In an interview she gave when she was 75, cited by the Jewish Women's Archive, she said her assets were: "a strong constitution, a devotion to duty and a big conscience," together with "a flair for organization" and "a pretty big capacity for righteous indignation."

It was this "righteous indignation," this anger at social injustice, that pushed Henrietta to take decisive action. She started the first American night school to provide English language instruction and vocational skills to Russian Jewish immigrants in Baltimore. She helped found the Jewish Publication Society and served as its first and, for a long time, only staff member, editing, writing and translating Jewish books. She was the first woman to attend the Jewish Theological Seminary in New York and impressed everyone with her studies, even though they didn't allow her – or any woman – to become a rabbi at the time.

It was Henrietta's decision to say Kaddish for her mother, which was criticized by some as something women didn't do, that inspired future Supreme Court Justice Ruth Bader Ginsburg to write these words: "Szold's plea for celebration of our common heritage while tolerating, indeed appreciating, the differences among us concerning religious practice is captivating. I recall her words even to this day when a colleague's position betrays a certain lack of understanding."

In 1912 Henrietta, determined to help families she saw starving and struggling without proper sanitation in the land that would become Israel, founded the charitable organization Hadassah with a simple mission to provide emergency care to infants and mothers there. That goal would expand its reach into offering advanced medical care for all through two world-class medical and research centers in Jerusalem and additional outreach programs. She served as its president until 1926. Henrietta's insistence that Hadassah serve all in need, regardless of race, ethnicity or nationality, earned Hadassah a nomination for the Nobel Peace Prize in 2005. In a land long roiled by conflict, Hadassah continues to serve as a model of cooperation, coexistence, comfort, and inclusion, with a diverse medical staff caring for a diverse group of patients.

Henrietta conceived of Hadassah as a charity run by women at a time when women had limited opportunities to work or make their voices heard; they wouldn't even have the right to vote nationally in America until 1920. As hundreds of thousands of women raised funds and put Hadassah's life-saving programs into action, they proved the power of women to effect change. As the power of Hadassah grew, so did the determination of the women of Hadassah to be heard, valued, and included as equals. Soon, in addition to fighting for advanced medical care, education, and youth development in Israel, the women of Hadassah became advocates for women's rights and social justice worldwide.

When Henrietta first came to Palestine, the barren land was dotted with a mix of natives from a variety of faiths, Jewish, Muslim, Christian, and Druze, as well as Jewish refugees escaping persecution in Russia and Europe. In the early 20th century, the land was ruled by the British Empire and tensions among Arabs, Jews, and the British government escalated. Henrietta saw the land as a home for all and supported Brit Shalom (meaning Covenant of Peace), founded in 1925, an organization dedicated to Arab-Jewish unity. Ever mindful of the need to save and help children in need, in 1934, she directed Youth Aliyah, an organization founded by Recha Freier in 1933, that rescued 11,000 Jewish children from the Holocaust.

Henrietta died before Israel became a state, but after her first visit she was keenly aware that a Jewish homeland might be the only salvation from the threats facing her people. Two decades before the Holocaust, she wrote in a letter: "I am more than ever convinced that if not Zionism, then nothing — then extinction for the Jew!"

Henrietta died at age 84 in the Hadassah Hospital she had helped build in Jerusalem. She never married or had children, but three years after the founding of the state of Israel, the country honored her as "the mother of Israel" by choosing the date of her death as their Mother's Day. A child she had rescued from the Holocaust said Kaddish for her.

She is buried in the Jewish Cemetery on the Mount of Olives in Jerusalem. Among the many things named for her are the Henrietta Szold Institute in Jerusalem and the Henrietta Szold prize, which Hadassah awarded to First Lady Eleanor Roosevelt in 1949. In 2007, Henrietta was inducted into the American National Women's Hall of Fame for her "84 years of social activism," including her rescue of more than 11,000 young people from the threats of Nazi Europe to pre-state Israel, and how that bold effort matched deeds to her often-repeated words: "make my eyes look toward the future."

Purim

Purim is a Jewish holiday that celebrates the courage of Queen Esther, who spoke up to save her Jewish community and became a model for others, like Henrietta. Esther lived in the 4th century BCE when King Ahasuerus of Persia ruled over many lands and people. This powerful King had a fierce temper. He executed his wife, Queen Vashti, when she didn't obey him. When he married Esther, she didn't tell him she was Jewish as she knew that could have put her in danger, especially after the king appointed Haman, a man who hated Jewish people, as his prime minister. When Esther's proud Jewish cousin, Mordechai, refused to bow to Haman, Haman convinced the king to call for killing all Jews on the 13th of Adar in the Jewish calendar. Now Esther had a big choice. She could have stayed quiet and safe. Instead, she decided to speak up and tell the king she was Jewish. The king loved Esther. He wanted to protect her and her people. It was too late to recall his order, but he sent out a new decree, giving Jewish people the right to defend themselves. The Jewish people fought back and on the next day, the 14th of Adar, they rested and celebrated. That's why Purim is celebrated on the 14th of Adar, which usually occurs in March.

People celebrate Purim by reading the Megillah, the story of Esther, sending Purim baskets of food, often including hamentashen, a holiday cookie that resembles Haman's three-cornered hat, to friends, giving charity, and putting on Purim shpiels — funny takes on the Purim story. When listening to the Megillah, it's traditional to use groggers — noisemakers — to drown out the name of Haman whenever it appears in the story. Purim is a festive holiday, a celebration of survival and of pride. Henrietta treasured an olive wood Purim scroll that she received in 1909 on her first visit to Palestine, which has since been included in an exhibition, "Daughter of Zion: Henrietta Szold and American Jewish Womanhood," presented by the Jewish Historical Society of Maryland. Three years later, Henrietta founded Hadassah, which is Esther's Hebrew name, on Purim in 1912. For Henrietta and the women of Hadassah, the queen's pride in her identity and the bravery she showed in asking justice from a king filled them with the courage to stand up to powerful forces to help their people – and all people.

Image provided by The Library of The Jewish Theological Seminary

Timeline

1860	Henrietta Szold (pronounced ZOHLD) is born in Baltimore, Maryland to Rabbi Benjamin Szold and his wife, Sophie Schaar Szold, on Dec. 21.
1881	More than two-and-one-half million Jews facing anti-Semitism and lack of economic opportunity in Eastern Europe immigrate to America over the next four decades.
1889	Henrietta establishes the first American night school to teach English and vocational skills to immigrants.
1893	Henrietta becomes the first and only editor for the Jewish Publication Society and translates, writes, edits, and oversees the publication schedule of books for more than 23 years.
1902	Henrietta excels in advanced Jewish studies at the Jewish Theological Seminary but is not allowed, as a woman, to become a rabbi.
1909	Henrietta makes her first trip to what was then called Palestine, part of the Ottoman Empire.
1912	Henrietta starts Hadassah, the first charity founded and run by women, with the mission to provide healthcare, food, and other assistance for all residents in Palestine, including Jews and Arabs. She serves as president until 1926.
1916	After Henrietta's mother's death, a male friend offers to say Kaddish, the prayer for the dead, as women at that time did not say Kaddish. Henrietta insists on doing it herself — an action that changes tradition and encourages other women to recite it as well.
1933	Adolf Hitler, head of the Nazi party, is appointed to lead the German government in January.
1933	Henrietta immigrates to Palestine and helps run Youth Aliyah, an organization that rescues and resettles 11,000 Jewish children from Nazi Europe.
1939	World War II begins on Sept. 1.
1945	Henrietta dies on Feb. 13 at age 84 in the Hadassah Hospital she helped build in Jerusalem. She is buried in the Jewish Cemetery on the Mount of Olives in Jerusalem.
1945	World War II ends on Sept. 2.
1949	Hadassah inaugurates the Henrietta Szold prize, which was given to First Lady Eleanor Roosevelt that year.
1952	Israel honors Henrietta by celebrating Mother's Day on the day that Szold died, which falls on the 30th of Shevat in the Hebrew calendar.
2005	Hadassah is nominated for the Nobel Peace Prize.
2007	Henrietta is inducted into the National Women's Hall of Fame in Seneca Falls, New York.

Bibliography

Henrietta never wrote an autobiography, but she did many interviews, wrote many letters, and had a handful of biographies written about her, including:

Fineman, Irving. *Woman of Valor: The Life of Henrietta Szold, 1860-1945*. Simon and Schuster, 1961.

Dash, Joan. *Summoned to Jerusalem: The Life of Henrietta Szold*. Harper & Row, 1979.

Hacohen, Dvora. *To Repair a Broken World: The Life of Henrietta Szold, Founder of Hadassah*. Translated by Shmuel Sermoneta-Gertel, Harvard University Press, 2021.

This exhibit, presented by the Jewish Historical Society of Maryland, provided a treasure trove of artifacts and articles including a *New York Times* article about Henrietta's rescue of children from the Holocaust:

Daughter of Zion: Henrietta Szold and American Jewish Womanhood. 9 Apr.-10 Dec. 1995, Jewish Museum of Maryland, Baltimore.

"Rescued Children Thank Miss Szold." The New York Times, 16 Feb. 1944, www.msa.maryland.gov/megafile/msa/speccol/sc3500/sc3520/013500/013568/pdf/nytimes16feb1944.pdf.

Other sources, including those for direct quotations, are as follows:

Jewish Women's Archive. "Biography: Henrietta Szold (1860–1945)." www.jwa.org/article/biography-henrietta-szold-1860-1945

Ginsburg, Ruth Bader. "Remarks at the Genesis Foundation Lifetime Achievement Award Ceremony." 4 Jul. 2018, Tel Aviv. Speech. www.supremecourt.gov/publicinfo/speeches/J.%20 Ginsburg %20Remarks%20Genesis%20Lifetime%20Achievement%20Award%20Tel%20Aviv%20 Israel%20July%204%202018%20(3).pdf.

National Women's Hall of Fame. "Henrietta Szold." www.womenofthehall.org/inductee/henrietta-szold.

Grigsby, Randy. *Hadassah Magazine*. "Henrietta Szold's Children." Jan. 2020. www.hadassahmagazine.org/2020/01/07/henrietta-szolds-children.

Thanks to Dr. Joe Goldblatt and his daughter Miriam for the letter from Justice Ruth Bader Ginsburg.

She knew she could be attacked or arrested at any time as she met secretly with crying parents, begging them to let their children go to a country they'd never seen to be cared for by Henrietta, whom they'd just met.